Following Jesus

Following Jesus

The Essentials of
Christian Discipleship

Andrew M. Randall

THE BANNER OF TRUTH TRUST

THE BANNER OF TRUTH TRUST

Head Office	*North America Office*
3 Murrayfield Road	PO Box 621
Edinburgh	Carlisle
EH12 6EL	PA 17013
UK	USA

banneroftruth.org

First published 2018
© Andrew M. Randall 2018
Reprinted 2020

*

ISBN
Print: 978 1 84871 824 1
Epub: 978 1 84871 825 8
Kindle: 978 1 84871 827 2

*

Typeset in 11/15 Adobe Garamond Pro
at The Banner of Truth Trust, Edinburgh

Printed in the USA by
Versa Press Inc.,
East Peoria, IL.

For Kay,

who daily helps me to follow Jesus,

and

for Colin & Laura,

who see him face to face.

Contents

Introduction

Vince Lombardi was one of the great American football coaches. He led the Green Bay Packers to five NFL championships in the space of seven years, as well as victory in the first two Super Bowls. The Super Bowl trophy is named after him. His biographer records one of the keys to his success:

> He began a tradition of starting from scratch, assuming that the players were blank slates who carried over no knowledge from the year before. He reviewed the fundamentals of blocking and tackling, the basic plays, how to study the playbook. He began with the most elemental statement of all. 'Gentlemen,' he said, holding a pigskin in his right hand, 'this is a football.'[1]

That great one-liner was Lombardi's way of reminding his players that the life and soul of the game lay in the basics. Success did not depend mainly on flashes of genius, but on getting the basics right most of the time.

The purpose of this book is to take you back to the basics of discipleship. At some point you, like the disciples of old, heard the call of Jesus to 'Follow me.' That may have happened recently, in which case I pray that God might use these pages to lay some solid foundations for a healthy and rich Christian life. It may have happened years ago, in which case this is a refresher course in what it means to be a disciple of Jesus.

[1] David Marannis, *When Pride Still Mattered: A Life of Vince Lombardi* (New York: Simon & Schuster, 1999), p. 274.

This book is shaped by three convictions. The first is that *love for Christ should shape our lives*. In Mark 14, a woman empties an alabaster flask of precious ointment over Jesus' head, pouring out this costly offering as an expression of her love and devotion to him. As those who have been purchased by Christ at the cost of his life, we are called to pour out every part of our lives for him. We are to love him with all that we are and have. That is why the chapters that follow address the practical, everyday things of the Christian life. Why do Christians emphasise the Bible so much? Is church really such a big deal? Is Jesus relevant to my everyday work? How should my faith affect my relationships? What am I to make of it when I suffer?

The second conviction that shapes this book is that *theology matters*. If we want to know about practical Christian living we must build on theological foundations, because there is nothing more practical than good theology. The way we live is always the product of what we believe. The more we know God, the more we will love him, the better we will honour him, and the more effectively we will serve him and others. Theological convictions are never far away in these pages, because if Christian living is not grounded in sound Christian doctrine, it will always degenerate into hard legalism on the one hand or sinful licence on the other. Both of these are life-denying and joy-killing. Gospel grace is the only soil in which glad and loving obedience grows. For a detailed biblical theology you'll have to look elsewhere, but I would recommend that you do, since 'theology' simply means the study of God and that is a subject for everyone.[2]

The third conviction that shapes this book is that *the gospel you have come to believe is not just the truth about religion, but the truth about everything*. It is what Francis Schaeffer used to describe as 'true

---

[2] For a reliable and readable introduction to theology, I would recommend R. C. Sproul, *Everyone's A Theologian* (Orlando, FL: Reformation Trust, 2014).

Truth' or 'total Truth'.[3] That means its implications stretch from one end of your week to the other, and into every aspect of your life. This book is a basic guide to what that means.

In the coming pages we'll cover a lot of ground, but we won't have the space to delve into each issue as deeply as we might like. In Appendix 3 you'll find a list of resources – one book for every chapter of this book – which can help you to delve more deeply into the truth you have come to believe and into the life of discipleship.

So with that introduction:

Ladies and gentlemen, this is a football...

ANDREW M. RANDALL
Larbert, Scotland
September 2018

---

[3] Francis A. Schaeffer, *Escape from Reason* (London: Inter-Varsity Fellowship, 1968), p. 21. See also Nancy Pearcey, *Total Truth: Liberating Christianity from its Cultural Captivity* (Wheaton: Crossway, 2005).

CHAPTER ONE

Following Jesus at His Call:
The Essentials of Faith

Now after John was arrested, Jesus came into Galilee, proclaiming the gospel of God, ¹⁵ and saying, 'The time is fulfilled, and the kingdom of God is at hand; repent and believe in the gospel.'

¹⁶ Passing alongside the Sea of Galilee, he saw Simon and Andrew the brother of Simon casting a net into the sea, for they were fishermen. ¹⁷ And Jesus said to them, 'Follow me, and I will make you become fishers of men.' ¹⁸ And immediately they left their nets and followed him. ¹⁹ And going on a little farther, he saw James the son of Zebedee and John his brother, who were in their boat mending the nets. ²⁰ And immediately he called them, and they left their father Zebedee in the boat with the hired servants and followed him.

²¹ And they went into Capernaum, and immediately on the Sabbath he entered the synagogue and was teaching. ²² And they were astonished at his teaching, for he taught them as one who had authority, and not as the scribes. – Mark 1:14-22.

Introduction: not seeing is believing

Which is faster: the speed of light or the speed of sound? It's not even close. Light blazes away at over 670 million miles per hour, leaving sound to wander along after it at a leisurely 761 miles per hour. If you watch from a distance as a man hits a fence post with a sledgehammer, you will see the impact long before you hear it.

I

But here is a strange fact: in the Christian life, the speed of sound is faster than the speed of light. We hear things before we see them.[1] When it comes to the great truths about life, death and the universe, God tells us before he *shows* us. He informs us of things we cannot know ourselves, he asks us to live for him even though we cannot see him, and he makes promises to us about the future. In the interval between hearing of these things and seeing them come to pass, he asks us to trust him.

This is why, at the most basic level, the Christian life is the life of faith. Faith comes from hearing, says Paul (Romans 10:17); and so, until we see God's promises completely fulfilled in the new heavens and the new earth, we walk by faith and not by sight (2 Corinthians 5:7). Faith is sometimes spoken of as some kind of general attitude of hopefulness or credulity, but this is not how the Bible uses the word. Christian faith is an active trust in *what God has said*, and a living of life on that basis. The Christian trusts now in what is not yet, and believes now in what he cannot see, but he does so always on the basis of what God has told him. This is how we can be assured of what we hope for and convinced of what we do not see (Hebrews 11:1). There will come a time when faith will turn to sight, but for now you and I are called to trust – which means believing what God says, obeying what God commands, and expecting what he promises.

In Mark 1:14-22, at the beginning of his public ministry, Jesus calls Simon and Andrew, James and John. They respond to the call by following him, and so their life of discipleship begins. That remains the beginning of *all* discipleship, and the reason you're reading this book is that at some point you heard the call of Christ on your life. By his grace you were given the ability to respond in faith, and so you too became his disciple. The gospel writers (Matthew, Mark, Luke and John) all record the calling of the first disciples, but even as

---

[1] The illustration is used by Mark Dever, *Nine Marks of a Healthy Church* (Wheaton: Crossway, 2004), p. 45.

they do so they ensure that Jesus remains the focus of our attention. So we see very clearly from these first disciples that faith, rather than being some kind of abstract quality ('I wish I had your faith') or a set of intellectual opinions ('Does God really care whether you believe all the right things?'), is all about *trusting a person*. Jesus calls, 'and immediately they left their nets and followed him' (Mark 1:18). No doubt at this point there was a lot they didn't know about this new preacher, but clearly they knew enough to know that they could trust him. It was the beginning of an amazing transformation of their whole lives. Ordinary fishermen would become the founders of a faith that would change the world.

In this chapter we will look at faith from three angles: trusting God is about learning as a disciple, loving as a disciple, and living as a disciple.

Learning as a disciple

Faith is about learning, since we have to learn something about Jesus in order to be able to have faith in him in the first place. But having taken that step, it's important to remember that we remain learners. The Bible speaks about coming to faith as being 'born again'. That means that when you come to trust in Christ for the first time you are, spiritually speaking, a baby. You need to learn to feed, talk, crawl, walk and everything else that babies learn to do. The Bible develops this image. Peter urges us, 'Like newborn infants, long for the pure spiritual milk, that by it you may grow up to salvation' (1 Peter 2:2). Paul tells us that his great desire is to 'present everyone mature in Christ', which he seeks to do by proclaiming Christ, warning everyone, and teaching with all wisdom (Colossians 1:28). So faith involves learning.

When Simon, Andrew, James and John responded to the call of Jesus by following him, it means that they became his disciples. This is what Jewish rabbis (religious teachers) did. They gathered groups of men who would sit at their feet and learn from them. In fact, the word 'disciple' means learner. So these men followed Jesus in order to learn from him. If you have followed them into the life of discipleship, then you have enrolled as a student and will not graduate until you die.

I want to suggest three practical aspects of this learning.

1. The centrality of the Bible

First, we need to recognise the centrality of the Bible. Faith is about believing *what God has said*, not just positive thoughts that come into our heads. The latter is not faith, but foolishness. Faith is about believing *what God has revealed*, and that means a faith that feeds constantly on the Scriptures (another name for the Bible). You cannot claim to trust God while rejecting or disregarding his word, which is why in the next chapter we'll be considering why the Bible is such a big deal for Christians. For now, just notice what Mark tells us: the first disciples left their fishing nets, followed Jesus to Capernaum and heard him speak in the synagogue, where they and all the people 'were astonished at his teaching, for he taught them as one who had authority' (Mark 1:22). That remains the experience of God's people today, as they open his word. They find that, through Scripture, Jesus speaks powerfully into their lives. They learn from him.

There are of course many other resources on the market – endless books, conferences, websites and YouTube videos – which claim to be able to help us learn about Christ. Many of them are good and helpful but many others are not, and as a young Christian you will need the advice of more mature believers to be able to tell the difference. Above all else, remember that everything must be tested against the Bible, which is our supreme authority. And never allow these other resources to distract you from your greatest need, which is to read God's word itself. Even the best of Christian resources exist only to help us to learn the Scriptures, so the best thing you can do is to read your Bible carefully and prayerfully. Paul reminds us: 'Let the word of Christ dwell in you richly' (Colossians 3:16). That is how we learn.

2. The centrality of the gospel

As we emphasise the Bible in our Christian learning, it naturally follows that we should recognise the centrality of the gospel. The gospel is the core message of the Bible, the good news of what God has done for us and for our salvation. This message of good news has implications for every aspect of our lives – which is the point of this book – but its central thrust can be given in a few words: Jesus died for our sins, rose again, and is Lord. We know this because Paul tells us in so many words what is 'of first importance' in the Christian faith and life: 'that Christ died for our sins in accordance with the Scriptures, that he was buried, that he was raised on the third day in accordance with the Scriptures, and that he appeared' to witnesses (1 Corinthians 15:3-11).

However, this does not mean that the gospel is the way to *become* a Christian, but you must then move on to something more advanced in order to *grow* as a Christian. The gospel is not only the way in to the Christian life, but the way *of* the Christian life. The command of Jesus to 'repent and believe in the gospel' (Mark 1:15) is a command for you to obey every day until you die. We grow in faith as we repent of our sins and believe in the gospel every day of our life. When we struggle in our faith, as we might sometimes do, it's not because there is something deeper that we are missing out on. It's because we have lost sight of the gospel or failed to follow its implications in some area of our lives. Sadly we have an in-built tendency to forget the gospel at every turn, slipping into patterns of faithless thinking and sinful living, so we need to re-learn the gospel every day. The great reformer Martin Luther, who was not known for beating about the bush, insisted that the core message of the gospel is

> the principal article of all Christian doctrine, wherein the knowl-
> edge of all godliness consists. It is most necessary, therefore, that

we should know this article well, teach it unto others, and beat it into their heads continually.[2]

As far as Christian discipleship is concerned, half the battle is simply keeping the message of the gospel front and centre in our minds.

I lived for a few years in Dundee which is home to the *R.R.S. Discovery*, the ship which Captain Robert Scott and Ernest Shackleton took to the Antarctic in 1901. One of the artefacts on display is a pair of snow goggles which Scott used. Essential for the prevention of 'snow blindness', these are clumsy wooden goggles which have his initials carved into the top, and a cross carved out at each eye for visibility. Throughout his expedition, Scott would have looked at the Arctic world through the lens of a cross. This is what we must learn to do, understanding both the meaning of history and the purpose of our own lives through the lens of the cross of Christ. We need to understand others through the lens of the cross, seeing them as sinners in need of a Saviour. We need to see our fellow Christians through the lens of the cross, as those for whom Christ died. We need to see ourselves through the lens of the cross, as precious souls purchased by the blood of Christ. We need to see our past through the lens of the cross, so that there is no place for pride because salvation is all of him and no place for shame because forgiveness is ours in him. We need to look to the future through the lens of the cross, as an opportunity to serve our crucified and risen Saviour. The gospel must be central in all things.

3. The centrality of the church

Thirdly, we must recognise the centrality of the church to our learning as disciples. Again we'll devote a later chapter to this. We benefit greatly from teachers whom God has called and equipped to preach his word. We also learn a great deal from other believers, and especially those who are more mature in the faith. One of the best things

[2] Martin Luther, *St Paul's Epistle to the Galatians* (Philadelphia: Smith, English & Co., 1860), p. 206 (English updated).

a new Christian can do is to befriend a few older, wiser Christians in their church and spend some time with them.

In all these ways we learn as disciples.

Loving as a disciple

But faith goes further. Faith involves a personal commitment at the level of the heart. The life of discipleship is not only about learning, but also about loving. Jesus' first disciples didn't follow him because they thought it would be an interesting intellectual adventure, but because they had heard the call to enter into a living relationship with him. In their case that meant being with him physically day by day, travelling with him, watching him, listening to him. It is fascinating to follow their journey. They are constantly amazed by Jesus, often puzzled by him, sometimes completely in awe of him, but what you cannot mistake is that his followers very quickly came to love him. These were men's men – mainly weather-beaten fishermen – but they were devoted to Christ as their leader and their Lord. They could see that he loved them, and in response they couldn't help but love him in a deep and life-changing way.

Christian faith has propositional content. It is clear and rational and coherent, and needs to be learned. But the life of faith goes far deeper than believing certain propositions. To believe in God is not Christian discipleship. To believe that Jesus was a good man is not Christian discipleship. Even to know that Jesus died for the sins of others is not Christian discipleship. Christian discipleship is what happens when you meet this man, and come to love, to trust and to follow him.

Love for Christ is not something pathetically emotional. It engages the emotions intensely, but it is something of great strength and deliberate commitment. Paul calls it 'a sincere and pure devotion to Christ' (2 Corinthians 11:3), which is a wonderful expression because it captures something of this intertwining of love, trust and following. We give ourselves to Christ in response to his giving of himself for us, and faith always carries this sense of personal investment in Christ.

This is why the mockery that our culture so often levels at 'faith' is so misguided. Faith is not about believing six impossible things before breakfast; or believing the opposite of whatever the evidence tells you; or even, as Mark Twain cynically suggested, 'believing what you know ain't so'.[3] Faith is believing *what you can't see* – and that is a very different matter, because sometimes there are very good reasons to believe what you can't see. In the end, faith makes sense because of who Jesus is, and our love and trust in him cannot be separated. That means we will respond to him in certain ways. What he says, we will accept. What he promises, we will believe. What he gives, we will receive. What he withholds, we will forego. What he commands, we will do. This is what it looks like to love Jesus from the heart.

Living as a disciple

It becomes increasingly clear, then, that as well as learning as a disciple and loving as a disciple, faith also involves living as a disciple. 'O it is a living, busy, active, mighty thing, this faith,' declared Martin Luther.[4] Believing in Jesus changes everything. His first disciples discovered that. After they responded to Jesus' call, their lives would never be the same again. Much had changed around them, but more fundamentally something had changed within them. Their whole outlook on life had been revolutionised, their perspectives and priorities had been transformed, and so they lived differently. This is how John Stott put it:

> Everywhere in the New Testament God's truth is something to be *done*, not something only to be believed. It carries with it

[3] Mark Twain, *Following the Equator: A Journey Around the World* (Hartford: American Publishing Company, 1897), p. 132.

[4] Martin Luther, 'Preface to the Epistle of St. Paul to the Romans', in *Luther's Works, Volume 35, Word and Sacrament I.*, ed. E. Theodore Bachmann (Philadephia: Fortress Press, 1960), p. 370.

demands, duties, obligations. The evangelical faith radically transforms those who believe and embrace it.[5]

The forgiveness of our sins is at the heart of the gospel, but it is not
the whole of the gospel. We don't just get saved from our sins and
then wait for heaven! The gospel introduces us to a whole new life.
It declares that God has acted to redeem his world, to introduce
his Kingdom in a new way, to establish and build his church, and
to prepare for the day when he will make all things new. God is at
work in his world, and he calls us to be a part of what he is doing.
Our problem is that we know and believe the gospel one moment,
and the next moment we live in ways that are completely inconsistent with that belief. So we celebrate God's free forgiveness, and
then hold grudges against others. We rejoice in God's generosity to
us, and then hoard possessions for ourselves. We are humbled and
happy to have our feet washed by Christ, and then fail to serve him
and others because we are too busy insisting on our own way. True
faith involves living as a disciple, which is another way of saying that
it involves the gospel impacting every part of our lives.

Tim Keller gives an illustration, which is really his wife Kathy's.
They used to live in apartment blocks in New York City which had
vending machines. Fairly often the coins would get jammed in the
machinery and nothing would happen. So you had to thump the side
of the machine, and thump it again, until eventually it spat out your
Coke. The life of the gospel can be like that. We receive the truth,
but we are slow to produce its fruit. So like Luther, we have to beat
the gospel into each other's heads continually. We hammer away, and
yet there are areas of our lives that seem to remain untouched. So
we keep hammering away until finally, with a nudge from the Holy
Spirit, the penny drops.

So I need to tell you, by way of fair warning, that the rest of this
book will basically hammer the side of the machine. We will take

---

[5] John Stott, *Make the Truth Known* (Leicester: IVP, 1983), p. 12 (emphasis
original).

the gospel and see how it looks when it is applied to different aspects of our lives. What does the gospel have to do with my work, my money, my relationships, my lifestyle?

This is about allowing the gospel to shape our lives. We are saved by grace through faith in Christ, but that faith in Christ comes with a commitment to a certain kind of life. He is not only our Saviour, he is our Lord, and his lordship is total. He must be first, and that means that every aspect of our life is to be surrendered to his rule. That does not mean that we're going to spend the rest of these pages compiling a long set of rules that Christians must obey if they want God to love them and approve of them. God *has* loved us, and chosen us to belong to him, not from anything in us but out of sheer love and mercy. That creates a completely different dynamic, as we seek to live for him in response to his amazing grace and goodness. Now the gospel becomes the driving force for a new life which we rejoice to pursue. We gladly surrender to him as the one we learn from, love and live for.

Conclusion

These are the basics of faith: to follow Jesus at his call, in love and in trust. We trust him for the forgiveness of our sins through his death on our behalf. We trust him for the gift of new life through his resurrection. We trust him to lead and love, guide and guard, provide and protect as he has promised. And we trust him, not because we have seen the fulfilment of all his promises, but because we have heard his word.

The speed of sound is faster than the speed of light. That is why, for now, we trust. That is the deepest foundation of Christian discipleship.

CHAPTER TWO

Following Jesus by the Book: The Essentials of the Bible

You, however, have followed my teaching, my conduct, my aim in life, my faith, my patience, my love, my steadfastness, [11] my persecutions and sufferings that happened to me at Antioch, at Iconium, and at Lystra – which persecutions I endured; yet from them all the Lord rescued me. [12] Indeed, all who desire to live a godly life in Christ Jesus will be persecuted, [13] while evil people and impostors will go on from bad to worse, deceiving and being deceived. [14] But as for you, continue in what you have learned and have firmly believed, knowing from whom you learned it [15] and how from childhood you have been acquainted with the sacred writings, which are able to make you wise for salvation through faith in Christ Jesus. [16] All Scripture is breathed out by God and profitable for teaching, for reproof, for correction, and for training in righteousness, [17] that the man of God may be competent, equipped for every good work.

[1] I charge you in the presence of God and of Christ Jesus, who is to judge the living and the dead, and by his appearing and his kingdom: [2] preach the word; be ready in season and out of season; reprove, rebuke, and exhort, with complete patience and teaching. [3] For the time is coming when people will not endure sound teaching, but having itching ears they will accumulate for themselves teachers to suit their own passions, [4] and will turn away from listening to the truth and wander off into myths. [5] As for you, always be sober-minded, endure suffering, do the work of an evangelist, fulfil your ministry. – 2 Timothy 3:10–4:5.

Introduction: the greatest and most enduring treasure

A young man by the name of Sami was driving on the outskirt of Beirut. It was not a good place to be at the time. He saw a suitcase lying beside the road, so he stopped the car. His wife Joy begged him not to go anywhere near it, but he was concerned that some-one might have lost something. As it turned out, he was right. Rather than containing the bomb that Joy had feared, the suitcase was crammed with banknotes. It also contained a name and con-tact details, and when they got home Sami called the number and spoke to a very relieved man. The suitcase had fallen from his car as he tried to flee the city. The evangelist Ravi Zacharias was with his friend Sami when the owner of the suitcase brought his family to meet him.

> As they sat in Sami's living room, completely overwhelmed, Sami said gently, 'You think you have recovered your treasure. Let me tell you how passing a treasure this is. With the fragile state of our country, this could become completely worthless overnight. Let me give you the greatest and the most enduring treasure you can ever have.' He handed them a copy of the Bible. It was a memorable moment as they held it in their hands. Was this real? Was this the word of God? Was this indeed the greatest treasure on earth, a light to their feet and a lamp to their path?[1]

If you have recently become a disciple of Jesus, you may still be wondering why Christians make quite such a big deal about the Bible. You get that it's important, but do Christians need to be quite so obsessed with it? The answer depends on knowing what the Bible is, why we need it, how it works and what it does. These are the questions we'll be exploring in this chapter.

It's amazing how often it's forgotten that the Bible is the foundation of everything that Christians believe. Take it away, and what we can know confidently about God amounts to this: the creation around us tells us that God is breathtakingly powerful, and

[1] Ravi Zacharias, *Deliver Us From Evil* (Dallas: Word Publishing, 1996), p. 153.

the conscience within us tells us that we have seriously offended him. That combination is not good news! If we want to know more about God – who he is, what he thinks, how we can relate to him – then we need the Bible to tell us. This is the source of our knowledge of him; this is where he speaks to us; and most of all, this is where we have a living encounter with him in the person of his Son.

What is it?

The most basic question of all to ask about the Bible is this: what is it? What are you holding when you hold your Bible? You may know by now that the Bible is a collection of sixty-six books, written by dozens of different authors over many hundreds of years. These books reflect the personalities and styles of their authors, the cultures in which they lived, and the reasons they were writing. There is history, poetry, law, prophecy, wisdom literature, correspondence and more. When these texts were written, their human authors exercised the same creative process of research and thought and composition that you would expect of any writing, and they consciously set out to write something truthful and compelling. Luke begins his gospel, for example, by assuring us that he has carefully investigated all the facts in order to set down 'an orderly account' so that we can have certainty that what we believe is true (Luke 1:1-4).

So when we claim, as we do, that the Bible is the word of God, we are not suggesting that its authors went into some kind of trance, or became mindless robots who were dictated to by God. They were fully involved in the process of writing. Nevertheless, one of the most startling features of the Bible is that, the more you come to know it, the more you realise that despite all the different authors, styles, eras and cultures, this is a single book. It runs to over a thousand pages in most editions, but in the most astonishing way every part of it dovetails with every other part to make one magnificent story.

The reason for this biblical consistency and unity is that, in another sense, the Bible is really a single book that was written by a single author. Paul insists that 'All Scripture is breathed out by God' (2 Timothy 3:16), which is an amazing claim. The Bible is not just inspired in the normal sense of being a great work, and not just *inspiring* in the sense that it moves people, but is *ex-spired* – which means *breathed out* by God. Dale Ralph Davis uses a great expression to describe what this means:

> ...every time one deals with the word of God one is dealing with the God whose word it is. The word of God is not some extraneous object out there for us to squeeze to our liking; rather it is always warm with the breath of God's own mouth.[2]

This is why the Bible is so special to Christians. It comes to us direct from the living God, and if we want to get anywhere in the Christian life, there is nothing more important than grasping this. We need to understand that even as Moses, David, Ezekiel, Luke, Paul and all the other Bible writers researched, investigated, thought and wrote, God was speaking through them. Although he wasn't *controlling* them like puppets, he was *guiding* them by the Holy Spirit in all that they did, so that what they wrote was God's word.

Simon Peter, in an important passage, draws the conclusion that 'no prophecy of Scripture comes from someone's own interpretation. For no prophecy was ever produced by the will of man, but *men spoke from God* as they were carried along by the Holy Spirit' (2 Peter 1:20-21). This is the astonishing claim: men spoke from God. If that is not true, then we have no foundation for our faith. If it is, then this book must hold a place in our hearts and in our lives that is uniquely significant and authoritative.

Ultimately we have to ask: is the Bible a collection of the loftiest human thinking straining from earth towards heaven, or is it God revealing himself from heaven to earth? On the first view, it's an

---

[2] Dale Ralph Davis, *The Wisdom and the Folly: An Exposition of the Book of First Kings* (Fearn, Ross-shire: Christian Focus, 2002), p. 161.

interesting historical artefact. On the second, what you're holding when you hold your Bible are the very words of the living God, speaking with absolute truthfulness and supreme authority. That is a rock-solid foundation for faith. There are many reasons to accept the Scriptures as truthful, but here we only have space to touch on the two most basic ones.

1. The Bible's testimony to the Bible

First, the Scriptures tell us that they are completely truthful. If that sounds like the most blatant case of circular reasoning you have ever heard, I plead guilty! But think about it. If God chooses to reveal himself to humanity, there is no higher authority which could ever confirm the truth he declares. The self-revelation of God can only ever be self-authenticating. John 8 contains a helpful parallel, when Jesus announces, 'I am the Light of the world.' The Pharisees (religious leaders of the day who rejected Jesus) complain that 'You are bearing witness about yourself', but Jesus insists that his own testimony about himself can be trusted. This is because he is in a different category to any other witness. If he is the Light of the world, how could anything else shed light on Light? Light is its own testimony because it's *by* light that we see. You get the sense that John loves the irony of it all, and records the scene almost playfully. Why do you think Jesus needs corroborating evidence? Is it possible for truth to lie? Is it possible for light to 'shed darkness'?

In the same way, if God provides the Scriptures to be our supreme authority, there is no higher authority to which the Scriptures can appeal for confirmation of what they say. Therefore, just as God asks us to believe what the Bible says about everything else, he asks us to believe what the Bible says about itself. This means that the only way to discover whether the Bible is true is to taste and see. Read it, and ask God to speak to you through it. For thousands of years, Christians approaching the scriptures with an open mind have experienced what their spiritual ancestors in Thessalonica experienced in the first century: 'And we also thank God constantly for this, that when you received the word of God, which you heard from us, you accepted it not as the word of men but as what it really is, the word of God, which is at work in you believers' (1 Thessalonians 2:13).

2. Jesus' testimony to the Bible

The second reason to accept that the Bible is authoritative is that Jesus did. He had the Old Testament and the gospels make it clear that, as far as he was concerned, 'it is written' was the end of the matter. Whatever the Bible said, God said; and so whatever the Bible said, Jesus affirmed. In this modern age in particular there has emerged the phenomenon of the person who claims to be a follower of Jesus and yet shows little interest in the Bible. This is a self-defeating position, since only through the Bible do we know anything of substance about Jesus. It is also contradictory, since Jesus himself affirmed that 'Scripture cannot be broken' (John 10:35). In reality, if we want to call ourselves disciples of Jesus, we need to accept his view of the Bible.

So to the question 'What is the Bible? We must answer that it is the living word of God. That means that it speaks into our lives with supreme authority. Ray Galea has a nice way of bringing across the implications of this: 'When I first began to read the Bible with an open mind as a young adult, I discovered that God and Ray Galea thought very differently on a lot of issues. One of us would have to change.'[3]

Given who God is, and who we are, we should expect that God's word is going to confront and challenge us in all sorts of ways. The key thing is to approach it with the right attitude, which is one of humble submission. The best advice I can give you about the Bible is this: settle it in your mind right now that, however much it confronts, shocks, puzzles, or irritates you, everything the Bible says is true. This is what Jesus believed, and to be a disciple is to learn from him.

---

[3] Ray Galea, *God is Enough* (Kingsford: Matthias Media, 2010), p. 117.

Why do we need it?

Maybe you're persuaded that the Bible is something special, but why is it quite so important to make this book a part of your life? We've seen that we can only know about God and his gospel with confidence if he has revealed himself to us, but it goes further because we saw in the last chapter that the Christian message is not just to be received and believed, but to be *lived*. When we encounter God we realise that one of us is going to have to change, and it's not him! Our faith is intended to transform us, and Paul explores the implications of that in 2 Timothy 3-4. Paul reminds Timothy that, as a Christian and as a church leader, he is going to have to swim against the prevailing current of the culture. Living in ungodly times, amidst ungodly people, Timothy is to be 'competent' and 'equipped for every good work'.

Paul uses two different forms of the same word in that final expression from 2 Timothy 3:17. To translate it literally, you would have to say something like: we are to be made 'completely complete' for every good work. God doesn't intend to make us *partly* complete for the *occasional* good work, but *completely complete* for *every* good work. That is a high calling, and it can only happen as the word of God is allowed to do its work in our lives.

In other words, the reason we need the Bible so much is because the Bible equips us to live the Christian life. As we feed regularly on God's word, we grow in faith from infancy to maturity. The believer stands or falls by the word of God. Feed on a steady diet of God's word, and you will grow in faith. Deprive yourself of God's word, and your faith will inevitably weaken and wither. This is a basic principle that has been borne out in the experience of millions: you will know God as a living presence in your life, and you will be renewed and transformed by him, to the extent that you spend time with him regularly in his word. That's why we need the Bible.

How does it work?

That also helps us to answer the next question: how does it work? How does the Bible make a difference in our lives? Many have assumed that it's a book of rules that are to be kept, or presents examples that are to be followed. On this view it works by showing us what to do and what not to do, and commanding us to get on with it. That is a recipe for hopelessness and frustration, because we don't have the power to get on with it. What we need is the presence and power of God in our lives in order to transform us. We need God himself, and the Bible gives him to us. Here God speaks to us, making a living relationship with him possible.

That gives rise to a crucially important principle: *the main way the Bible equips us for every good work is not by telling us what to do for God, but by telling us what God has done for us.* Read that sentence again, as often as you need to, until it sinks in. The Bible doesn't give us good advice but good news, and there is a world of difference between the two. The whole Bible is one huge story about what God has done to redeem a people for himself for eternity. That means it is all about Jesus Christ: the promise that he would come, the preparation for his coming, the event itself, and then everything that follows from it. Old Testament and New, every page is about him. That was his own understanding. On the first Easter Day, the risen Christ walked with two men on the road to Emmaus; and 'beginning with Moses and all the Prophets, he interpreted to them in all the Scriptures the things concerning himself' (Luke 24:27).

An Anglican bishop called Christopher Chavasse once suggested that the whole Bible is like a portrait of Christ. The four gospels paint in the main figure in the foreground: here we see Christ most clearly in focus. The Old Testament is the background, leading towards and drawing attention to the central figure. The letters of the New Testament are the clothing on that figure, which explain and describe him.

And then, while by our Bible reading we study the portrait as a great whole, the miracle happens! The Figure comes to life! And, stepping from the canvas of the written word, the everlasting Christ of the Emmaus Story becomes Himself our Bible teacher to interpret to us in all the Scriptures the things concerning Himself.[4]

The Bible points us to Christ, and by showing us his greatness and his excellence, his glory and his love, it exposes everything else we might choose to live for as the worthlessness and folly it really is. Instead, as Christ expands in our vision, and as our hearts are captivated by him, we are made increasingly complete and ready for every good work. As we walk with him closely, his character comes to shape ours. As we spend time with him every day, he begins to have a daily impact upon us. Over time, through the Bible's work in us, we see him more clearly, we love him more deeply, and we resemble him more closely.

What does it do?

So what should we expect to be happening in that process? In other words, what does the Bible do in our lives? Paul sets that out for us in a bit of detail in 2 Timothy 3. In the first place, the Bible is God's normal vehicle for bringing saving faith. The Scriptures are 'able [or powerful] to make you wise for salvation' (verse 15). There-fore, what the unbeliever needs more than anything is to read the Bible and encounter Jesus here by the power of the Holy Spirit. Paul makes clear in Romans 10 that 'faith comes by hearing, and hear-ing through the word of Christ'. God speaks through his word, to bring life to the spiritually dead. In this regard, a young man called Victor Nance was once imprisoned for selling drugs in Mississippi. After a year in Parchman, the state penitentiary, he asked to speak to a pastor and led him to a large oak tree which he called 'the tree of

---

[4] These remarks are recorded at John R. W. Stott, *Christ the Controversialist* (London: Tyndale, 1970), p. 104.

life'. He explained that a fellow inmate had given him a New Testament soon after he entered the prison, and out of sheer boredom he had sat under the tree every day reading it. The pastor recalls:

> it was there through the reading of God's Word that he became a Christian. Victor wanted to talk to me about his experience to be sure he had actually expressed saving faith in Jesus Christ, and I can assure you he had done just that. He was brought to faith through the witness of no one, only through the life-giving Word of God.[5]

Victor was brought to faith through the witness of no one, only through the life-giving Word of God.

The Scriptures truly are able to make you wise for salvation through faith in Christ Jesus.

But just as we saw in the last chapter that the gospel not only creates faith but grows it, so it's the same Bible that both makes us wise for salvation and brings us to maturity in Christ. There are specific things the Bible does in our lives. If I can rearrange the order of Paul's words slightly to show the logical flow:

> All Scripture is breathed out by God, and in order to make us completely complete for every good work, all Scripture is profitable for teaching, for reproof, for correction, and for training in righteousness.

So Scripture is useful, first, for teaching. Without it, we develop false understandings of God, the world, ourselves and our lives. For example, if we haven't learned from the Bible that this world is passing away but the things of God are eternal, we will be much more vulnerable to the lure of materialism. If we haven't seen how the nature of grace shapes the whole of life, we will be much more likely to snap back when someone insults or hurts us. Scripture teaches us what is true and what matters.

Secondly, the Bible is useful for reproof (rebuke or reprimand). False teaching needs to be rejected, and false living needs to be

[5] W. Wilson Benton Jr., 'The Biblical Basis of Pastoral Ministry', in *Totally Sufficient: The Bible and Christian Counselling*, ed. Ed Hindson and Howard Eyrich (Fearn, Ross-shire: Christian Focus, 2004), pp. 225-226.

rebuked. Without this we would remain comfortable in our sin. We live in ways which harm us, hurt others, damage our relationship with God – and we don't care. The Bible rebukes us, confronting us with the seriousness of our sin, making us feel its shame, and showing us how it doesn't fit with the new life that we've been given in Christ. If you've ever seriously engaged with the Bible, you will know something of that sense of a spotlight that is on your heart, exposing you. Of course, the reason God brings your sin to light in this way is so he can deal with it in grace and restore you to closer fellowship with him.

Thirdly, Paul tells us that the Bible is useful for correction. Given that we do sin, we need to be redirected from wrong to right paths. Where a bone is broken, we say that it is no longer 'true' or straight. It needs to be 'corrected' or re-set, so that it becomes realigned to everything else and can fulfil its proper function once more. In the same way, things go wrong in us at a moral and spiritual level. Even as we pursue godliness, things break and become misaligned, and need to be corrected. J. B. Phillips translated this as: 'All Scripture… is useful… for re-setting the direction of a man's life.'

Fourthly and finally, Scripture is useful for training in right-eousness. Remember that one of the reasons we need the Bible is because Christian faith is meant to transform our lives. Paul tells us here that it's through the Bible that we develop godly, Christ-like character. It is through the Bible that we learn how to live for God.

In all these ways, the Bible is essential in the life of the believer. It is the primary way in which God builds us up in faith, and the primary way in which he guides us through life. This is the air that Christians breathe.

So what?

So what? What difference does this make to you as a new Chris-tian, or as a Christian taking stock of your discipleship? I hope that the main practical implication is very obvious. One of the greatest needs of all disciples of Jesus, at every stage of our Christian life, is to get the Bible into our lives at every opportunity. To start with, make sure that you have your own copy of the Bible. Be aware that different translations of the Bible take slightly different approaches. Some (like *The Message* or the *New Living Translation*) are fairly loose translations, but can sometimes bring across the impact of the Bible's teaching in helpful ways. They're a good supplement, but your main Bible should be one which translates the text a little more closely and carefully. The *English Standard Version*, the *New Revised Standard Version*, the *Holman Christian Standard Bible* and the *New International Version* are all reliable.

Once you have your Bible, take some time to get to know it. If you find it helpful to underline verses that speak powerfully to you, or to scribble notes in the margin, go ahead and do it. If your Bible has cross-references in the middle of the page, footnotes, and a concordance at the back, have a look at these and learn how they work. (Often there's a section at the front explaining them.) Some Bibles have helpful articles explaining the historical context for different books, or maps which help you to understand the flow of the story better. It's also well worth learning the order of the sixty-six books of the Bible by heart, so that you can find your way around it easily. I have an appalling memory. I can't remember what I had for breakfast this morning, but even I have been able to memorise the books of the Bible, so I'm sure you can with a little effort.

Next, if you've recently become a Christian, one of the single most important things in your life right now is to make sure that you're part of a church which is utterly committed to the complete truthfulness of God's word, and utterly committed to teaching it faithfully. Too many Christians choose their church on the basis of the worship style, or the personality of the minister, or other things that are ultimately not important. What you need is a steady diet of solid Bible, and that should determine your choice of church more than anything else. In the verses quoted above Paul is writing to Timothy as an older minister to a younger one, and so his words tell us a great deal about what a preaching ministry should look like. We should be coming to church ready and eager to engage seriously with God's word. And as we come, we should expect to be taught, rebuked, corrected, and trained in righteousness as we are consistently pointed to the glory and grace of Christ in the gospel.

Of course, it's possible that there may not be a good Bible-teaching church near to you. Sadly, many churches today pay scant regard to the authority of God's word. It's possible that God might intend for you to be part of such a church in order to be a witness to others, and to encourage a more biblical ministry, but you should think long and hard before you commit to do so as a young Christian. Your need of Christian nurture is very great.

Be aware also, however, that Christians are not just to delegate the task of putting the Bible to work in their lives to their preachers. It's the mark of infancy if you always need someone else to find your food, cook it and chop it up into little bits. Before long, you expect even a small child to begin to feed himself. So while the Sunday-by-Sunday preaching of God's word is hugely important, it cannot replace commitment to regular personal Bible study. If anything, good preaching should whet our appetites and send us home eager to explore more of the Bible's goodness. We should come to see more clearly how important it is to spend time with God in his word, how much we need it, and how powerful and sufficient it is to equip us for a life of Christian discipleship.

Of course, the Bible can be an intimidating book for a young, or even not-so-young Christian. It's long, and parts of it are quite complex, and sometimes it can be hard to see just what you're meant to be getting from it. The fact that even Peter wrote about Paul's letters that 'There are some things in them that are hard to understand' (2 Peter 3:16) is a great comfort to many of us! Remember, though, that *all* Scripture is useful to teach, rebuke, correct and train in righteousness. And remember that the Bible reveals its truths, not to the clever, but to the humble and obedient. We *understand* God's word only when we first *stand under* it, acknowledging its authority over us. But when we do that, the Holy Spirit himself is our teacher, and opens our minds to receive what God has for us.

Be aware also that we can all benefit from help. It's certainly possible just to read your Bible and learn from it, but I have been a Christian literally for as long as I can remember and I still find it helpful to use simple daily Bible reading notes. There are many notes and devotional books available, so find something that suits you and stick with it. Set aside time for Bible reading and prayer each day. Don't worry about starting small if this is all new to you, but ask the Lord to increase your appetite for his word. Over time, as you learn to enjoy God's word more, and as you want to respond to him in prayer (which we'll think about in Chapter 4), this part of your life should naturally grow. Beware of legalism, and always remember that your standing before God does not depend on your performance. You're not saved by having a daily quiet time with God, but by the finished work of Christ. Nonetheless, we're called to live as Christians every day, and that means we need to be prepared and resourced every day. You feed your body several times daily. Take time to feed your soul.

There are a few final things we can do to supplement that basic diet of personal Bible study and regular preaching ministry. We can make sure that we take every opportunity to study the Scriptures. If your church has an evening service, you have a second opportunity on each Lord's Day (Sunday) to learn from God's word, as well as an opportunity to frame the day with worship morning and evening.[1] Your church may well run Bible studies, home groups,

---

[1] For more on the benefits of attending morning and evening services, see David Campbell, *The Lord's Day: Why Go to Church Twice on Sundays?* (Leominster: Day One Publications, 2015).

or midweek meetings, and these are often further opportunities to build the Bible into the normal rhythm of your life. These things can be supplemented by other resources, like Christian books and conferences, which help us to understand the Bible more. And one of the best ways to give the Bible a firm foothold in your life is to take the time to learn by heart parts of the Scriptures which are especially significant or helpful.

Conclusion: a steady diet

Different things will suit different people, but if we are to live a consistent life of Christian discipleship, we need a consistent diet of God's word. We need to be turning daily to this word of God – coming to us warm with the breath of God's own mouth – and we need to be praying:

> Lord, thank you for your word – the greatest and most enduring treasure I could ever have. Speak to me through it, by your Holy Spirit. Help me to see how this passage contributes to the whole Bible's picture of Christ. Show me how it displays his glory, and makes clear what he has done for his people. What are you teaching me today? How are you rebuking me in these verses? Where are you correcting me in this? How are you training me in righteousness? Father, shape me, that I might be made completely complete, equipped and eager to do all you ask of me. Make me someone who not only learns the gospel, and loves the gospel, but someone who is equipped to live the gospel – for my joy, and for your glory.

CHAPTER THREE

Following Jesus in Community: *The Essentials of Church*

Therefore remember that at one time you Gentiles in the flesh, called 'the uncircumcision' by what is called the circumcision, which is made in the flesh by hands – [12] *remember that you were at that time separated from Christ, alienated from the common-wealth of Israel and strangers to the covenants of promise, having no hope and without God in the world.* [13] *But now in Christ Jesus you who once were far off have been brought near by the blood of Christ.* [14] *For he himself is our peace, who has made us both one and has broken down in his flesh the dividing wall of hostility* [15] *by abolishing the law of commandments expressed in ordinances, that he might create in himself one new man in place of the two, so making peace,* [16] *and might reconcile us both to God in one body through the cross, thereby killing the hostility.* [17] *And he came and preached peace to you who were far off and peace to those who were near.* [18] *For through him we both have access in one Spirit to the Father.* [19] *So then you are no longer strangers and aliens, but you are fellow citizens with the saints and members of the household of God,* [20] *built on the foundation of the apostles and prophets, Christ Jesus himself being the cornerstone,* [21] *in whom the whole structure, being joined together, grows into a holy temple in the Lord.* [22] *In him you also are being built together into a dwelling place for God by the Spirit. –* Ephesians 2:11-22.

Introduction: making connections

Modern Western culture has come to be characterised by two strange paradoxes. The first is that we are more connected than ever, and yet at the same time more isolated than ever. Urbanisation has brought people physically closer together, and technology has created a global village. The smartphone has become so central to our lives that many of us can hardly breathe if we're separated from it for more than a few seconds. In that sense we are hardly ever disconnected. So why are we also more lonely and isolated than ever? Why are we so lacking any sense of the shared life which is the essence of community? Even where a family shares a home, why are their eyes so often glued to their individual screens (phones, tablets, TVs) rather than turned towards one another? Technology has brought astonishing advances and advantages, but are we not left with an uneasy sense that something important has been lost along the way? This is the first paradox: we are more connected, yet more isolated, than ever.

The second is that we feel more individualistic than previous generations, while also feeling thoroughly depersonalised. One of the defining characteristics of the modern West is rampant individualism. More and more, I come to think of 'who I am' in terms of myself-isolated-from-context, rather than myself-as-part-of... a family, a church, a community, a nation, a world. Life is all about self-expression, following my dreams and being who I want to be. My culture tells me constantly to be who I am – more than that, to be whoever I choose to be – and it promises to treat me accordingly. The advertisers know that there is a desire deep within me to be recognised personally and treated individually, and so they promise that their product will tailor itself to me and shape itself around me. Yet these are adverts being broadcast not just to me but to millions, and somehow it all rings hollow. In practice, the same culture that tells me to be an individual refuses to treat me like one.

I'm categorised in this way. I'm analysed in that way. I have to tick boxes on forms where none of the options applies to me. It must be one of the great ironies of history that our rampant individualism has so shaped our society as to squash individuality. I find myself being processed through systems that feel like they've been designed by other systems. (Have you even tried to phone your insurance company lately? Is that an experience to make you feel valued as a person? 'To make changes to your policy, press four…')

Wouldn't it be wonderful if we could find a place where both our individuality and our connectedness would be genuinely recognised and affirmed? What if there were a place where we would be respected, and listened to, and addressed as people, with dignity – but a place where we could also know that we are truly part of something bigger, standing alongside others, supporting and being supported, sharing in joy and in sorrow? Wouldn't it be thrilling to discover that individuality and community don't have be traded against each other, but can flourish and be made complete in one another?

It is often overlooked, but one of the most precious gifts that God gives to us in the gospel is the gift of the church. I don't mean a building, a denomination or even an event that happens on a Sunday. I'm talking about a community of individuals who trust in Christ. When we come to faith, we are joined with all other believers in the church throughout the world, and we are intended to take our place within one local church community. As one pastor has pointed out, 'Every single picture of what it means to be a believer in the New Testament is a corporate picture. We constitute a body under one head, a nation under one king, a flock under one shepherd, a building under one coping stone.'[1] To be a Christian is to belong to the church, and in that sense the church is essential to life as a believer.

[1] Peter White, *The Effective Pastor* (Fearn, Ross-shire: Christian Focus, 2002), p. 187.

As a young Christian, it will help you enormously if you under-stand as quickly as possible that those who come to faith (chapter 1) on the basis of the Bible (chapter 2) become part of the church (chapter 3). Being a disciple means, not just following Jesus, but following Jesus in community. So what does it look like to belong to a local church? What does it mean to belong to the worldwide church? And why does it matter quite so much?

Consider yourself… one of the family

As a Christian, you need to consider yourself… one of the family. (If you know the musical *Oliver*, you'll have the tune in your head for the rest of the day. You're welcome.) The church is the family of God's people. In fact, one of the most powerful images the New Testament uses to describe what God does for us in the gospel is adoption: we are adopted into the family of God.

Part of the background to Jesus' life and ministry is the long-standing separation between Jews and Gentiles (Gentiles being non-Jews). This separation was partly because, for very good reasons, God had commanded his people to keep themselves separate from the surrounding world. Yet in Ephesians 2:11-22, Paul rejoices that through the gospel God has simultaneously achieved two amazing results: he has reconciled us to himself, but in the process he has also united us to one another. Those who were separate are now brought together. Those who were divided by walls of hostility are now united. Those who were two people have become one people. He emphasises repeatedly that God has made all other differences of background and culture irrelevant.

The basis of this unity is Jesus Christ. Verse 20 is important: the household of God is 'built on the foundation of the apostles and prophets, Christ Jesus himself being the cornerstone'. The corner-stone is like the foundation of the foundation – the fixed point with which everything else must be aligned. If you are in line with the cornerstone, you are in the right place. If you are not in line with the cornerstone, it doesn't matter how many other stones you are in line with, and it doesn't matter how impressive a stone you are – you are in the wrong place and you are undermining the building. Jesus Christ is the cornerstone, so that it is 'in Christ' (verse 21) that the whole structure is joined together and can grow into what God intends it to be.

So the basis of our unity is not that we belong to the same culture, wear the same clothes, speak the same language, like the same songs or belong to the same denomination. The basis of Christian unity is not that we're like each other, or even that we like each other. It's not that we'll do our best to agree and get along with each other and everything will be lovely. God's church is built on the basis that we trust in the same Saviour, bow to the same King and follow the same Lord. Where that happens, he makes us one. All who are trusting in Christ are united to Christ, and that means that we are all united to one another too.

If you are trusting in him and seeking to follow him, consider yourself one of the family. That is both a command and an invitation. It's a command in the sense that this is not an optional extra, but part of your commitment of faith. This is how someone has put it.

> We are not saved individually and then choose to join the church as if it were some club or support group. Christ died for his people and we are saved when by faith we become part of the people for whom Christ died.[2]

So membership of a church community is an essential part of being a disciple of Jesus.[3]

This is rapidly disappearing, but in the past churches have often encountered the problem of traditionalism. People have attended, not because of a living faith in Christ, but because of a family or cultural tradition. In response, many people have been keen to

---

[2] Tim Chester and Steve Timmis, *Total Church* (Nottingham: IVP, 2007), p. 37.
[3] For more on this, see Sam Allberry, *Why Bother With Church?* (New Malden: Good Book Company, 2016).

point out that 'going to church doesn't make you a Christian'. This is true. Unfortunately, some have bizarrely concluded that being a Christian doesn't mean you have to go to church. I can worship God on the hills, on the golf course, in my boat... That conclusion is completely misconceived. In this, as in many areas of the Christian life, the question is not what we have to do, but what we get to do. If we understand the gospel, and if we read the Bible with an obedient spirit, we will understand that God intends for us to follow him together. If you had suggested to any of the New Testament writers that an individual Christian might choose to live without any commitment to a specific church family, they would have looked at you like you were from another planet. 'What's an individual Christian?' they would have asked. The whole idea is completely alien to biblical thought.

So considering yourself part of the family is a command, but it is also a wonderful invitation. It's an invitation in the sense that you are being told that you have a place here. This is your community. You're a citizen, says Paul (verse 19). In other words, you belong. You have all the privileges and protections of citizenship. Then he changes the image, and makes it much more personal: we are 'members of the household of God'. We are all part of one extended family, living a shared life. That is what community is – this experience that is so lacking in our society today. It's the sharing of life. If we think that belonging to a church means sitting in the same building once a week and maybe saying hello in the car park, we're a million miles from the picture Paul is painting. He is speaking about people who live, together, a single shared life.

Francis Chan tells a tragic story about a man who started to attend his church in California. A former gang member, heavily tattooed and rough around the edges, he was curious to see what church was like and he had a genuine interest in Jesus. A few months later he stopped going, so the pastor went to speak with him and asked if there was something wrong. This was his response: 'I had the wrong idea of what church was going to be like. When I joined the church, I thought it was going to be like joining a gang. You see, in the gangs we weren't just nice to each another once a week – we were family.'[4]

How tragic that there was a greater sense of community in a biker gang than in the church of Jesus Christ. That is a sign that something has gone badly wrong in the church. Disciples of Jesus are eternally united to one another in the deepest possible way, and we need to make that real in practice rather than just speaking about it in fine-sounding words. We need to see ourselves, not as lone rangers, but as musketeers: all for one, and one for all. We need to invest heavily in relationships with others in the local church community.

Let me add one more thing. Most churches have a formal membership structure. Sadly, some Christians have been infected by our culture's allergy to commitment and are reluctant to become members in this formal sense. This is a mistake. Church membership is a sensible thing for various practical reasons, but it's also an important way to commit yourself publicly to be there with and for your fellow-members. It says that you're serious about following Jesus as part of his people, and it says that you have the humility to submit to the guidance and discipline of the leaders God has appointed for his church. I urge you to become a member of your church. I hope that church will have a sensible, biblically-shaped leadership structure, with elders and ministers who love the Lord and teach the gospel. If so, wise Christians gladly submit to their leadership.

The importance of body-building

That brings us to the importance of body-building. If we are all part of a larger body, then it's important that each of us plays our part in building up that body. Paul puts it quite starkly: in Christ

[4] Francis Chan, *Forgotten God* (Colorado Springs: David C. Cook, 2009), p. 152.

'we, though many, are one body… and individually members one of another' (Romans 12:5). That's a radical thought: as a follower of Jesus, you belong to his people and are therefore duty-bound to seek the good of the whole church.

This is not easy because one of the glories and challenges of the church is that it consists of all people who are trusting in Jesus – whoever they are, whatever their personality, whatever their background and whatever their issues. They say you can choose your friends but you can't choose your relations: in the church they are one and the same, and you can't choose them there either! That means hard work. Let me ask: is your family a haven of undisturbed tranquillity and harmony at all times? Living together in God's family is an immense privilege, but it takes a serious commitment to overcome those things that come between us and would drive us apart. It takes a constant return to the gospel of grace. It takes humility towards self, thankfulness towards God and compassion towards others. If Christ has broken down dividing-walls of hostility, who are we to rebuild them?

So part of Christian discipleship is about thinking, carefully and deliberately, about how you can help to build up the body. What part can you play? How can you serve? Where could you be an encouragement to someone? How could you help someone practically? If you ask yourself these questions consistently, then whether you've ever thought of yourself as a body-builder before or not, this is what you will become.

What churches do and why they do it

So what should the life of a church fellowship look like, and what is your part in it? We don't have space to consider this in detail, but it's worth thinking through what we do in our churches and why.

Some time ago while I was reading a book about preaching, I was challenged by a section that was called 'What if God showed up this

Sunday?'⁵ Ask yourself: what if God himself were to guarantee that he would visit your church in person this Sunday? What if he were to promise that he would turn up in all his blazing glory and bring to your congregation a message, directly from his own lips, speaking directly into your circumstances and addressing your deepest needs? How would you respond? Would you come along if you could spare the time? Would you sing his praise half-heartedly? Would you complain about how long the service lasted? Would you spend time weighing up whether to agree with God's 'opinion' or not?

Or would you do anything – give anything – sacrifice anything – to be there? Would you not prepare yourself for this momentous event, coming in sorrow for your sin and in longing for greater holiness? Would you not recognise this as an astonishing act of kindness and condescension on God's part, and an amazing privilege for you to be there? And as you listened, would you not hang on his every word, and believe him unhesitatingly, and obey him gladly, and rejoice in the knowledge that God himself had come to you and spoken to you? Would you not be humbled, and thankful, and changed by the encounter?

Yet this is exactly the position you and I are in Sunday by Sunday as we meet with God's people. The book that we open together is the word of God. Where it is read reverently and proclaimed faithfully, God himself is personally present with us by his Holy Spirit. He speaks to us words which he breathed out long ago, but which were written for us.

1. Sunday services

Please trust me when I tell you, as a minister, that Sunday services are the life and soul of the local church. It's so important for you to be fully committed to being there week by week. Hebrews 10:24-25 makes clear that failure to attend church regularly is simply disobedience:

⁵ Phillip Jensen and Paul Grimmond, *The Archer and the Arrow* (Kingsford: Matthias Media, 2010), p. 19.

> And let us consider how to stir one another up to love and good works, not neglecting to meet together, as is the habit of some, but encouraging one another, and all the more as you see the Day drawing near.

Of course there may be times when you're ill, but church should take priority over all other distractions. There will also be times when you're away on holiday, and these are golden opportunities to find fellowship with brothers and sisters in other parts of the country or the world. In the internet age, a little advance research will usually let you identify a Bible-believing church which you can visit on holiday, and doing so will enrich your faith and expand your view of God's church.

But whenever you're at home, make church your priority. Don't commit to other things on a Sunday which will distract you from the profound blessings of sharing with your fellow Christians. Everything else you can do on other days of the week. On Sunday you need to receive the food of God's word. A well thought through church service should lead you into God's presence together with his people, call on you to exalt his glory in praise, encourage you to confess your sins, assure you of your forgiveness through the gospel, and help you to express your dependence on God in prayer. At the heart of the service, a well prepared sermon should lay before you a feast of biblical truth. Why would you miss this? So, as you wouldn't go without meals, don't go without church. And don't underestimate the impact it can have on your life if you walk into church Sunday by Sunday prepared for an encounter with the living God through his word.

Moreover, never underestimate how much you encourage others just by being there, or discourage them by being absent. You need the help and support of your brothers and sisters in Christ, and they need yours. The Bible makes many commands about how we should love one another, serve one another, encourage one another, comfort one another and so on. You cannot obey those commands unless you are meeting with your fellow Christians week by week.

2. Baptism

The church has also been commanded to perform Christian baptism. Baptism is what we call a sacrament, which means it is a sign pointing us to the grace of the gospel, and it is a seal (like a seal on a letter) by which God affirms that the promises of the gospel are coming from him to us. Baptism is the sacrament of entry into the Christian church, pointing to the cleansing from sin which is offered to us in the gospel.

Bible-believing people take different views on some aspects of baptism. Some Christians (and I'm one of them) believe that baptism should be administered to everyone who enters the visible church, whether by conversion or by birth. That means that we should baptise new converts who have never been baptised before, and the children of believers.[6] What this would mean for you as a new believer is that, if you were baptised as a child, you should give thanks to God that the gospel promises which were held out to you in your baptism have been fulfilled in your life. In most churches the next step would be for you to profess your faith, either to the elders or publicly in a church service, and be admitted to the Lord's Supper (see next point below). If on the other hand you have never been baptised before, you should speak to your pastor about being baptised now.

Other Bible-believing churches take the view that baptism should only be administered to those who have consciously repented and believed, and that it should always be performed by full immersion. It will be important for you to discuss these issues with your pastor, remembering that they are secondary issues and that people who disagree with each other in these things should nonetheless affirm one another as brothers and sisters in Christ.

[6] For an explanation of the theology and practice of infant baptism I would recommend Bryan Chapell, *Why Do We Baptize Infants?* (Phillipsburg: Presbyterian & Reformed, 2006) or John Murray, *Christian Baptism* (Phillipsburg: Presbyterian & Reformed, 1980).

3. The Lord's Supper

Shortly before his death, Jesus instituted a meal known as the Lord's Supper (sometimes called communion). This is also a sacrament, or a sign and seal of the gospel. If baptism is the sacrament of entry into the church, the Lord's Supper is the sacrament of belonging. That means this is a meal for Christians only, and the Bible confirms that participating in it requires self-examination and conscious saving faith in Jesus (1 Corinthians 11:23-29). We look beyond the symbols of bread and wine to what they signify, namely the body of Jesus broken for us and the blood of Jesus shed for us.

The Lord's Supper goes beyond mere symbolism, however. We believe that, as we receive this meal, the Lord Jesus meets with us in a special way by the power of his Holy Spirit. This is no magic ceremony, and the Lord's Supper does no good to anyone unless they have faith in Christ crucified and risen. But in ways that go beyond our understanding, we believe that God's Spirit works in our spirits as we receive the bread and wine, to nourish and strengthen us in our faith. The way one great Scottish preacher of old put it was that, although the Lord's Supper doesn't convey to us anything different from the gospel, we 'get the same thing better' than before. Somehow, through it, we get 'a better hold of Christ' than we would have without it.

> Even though Christ is the same in Himself, yet the better hold you have of Him, the surer you are of His Promise. The Sacraments are appointed that I may have Him more fully in my soul, that I may have the bounds of it enlarged, and that He may make the better residence in me.[7]

So the Lord's Supper is a special gift to believers, which we should cherish greatly.

Jesus commanded his followers to observe this meal regularly until he returns. Some churches do this weekly, others less frequently.

[7] Robert Bruce, *The Mystery of the Lord's Supper*, ed. T. F. Torrance (Fearn, Ross-shire: Christian Focus, 2005), pp. 59-60.

Your church will probably have a pattern of regular communion services. Take note of it so that you can come to church that day prepared in your mind and heart for what you will be doing. The command of Jesus is that, through this, we are to 'remember him' (Luke 22:19). There's a kind of joyful solemnity to communion – or a solemn joy, if you prefer to look at it that way. It's a solemn occasion because here we reflect deeply on the terrible cost of our salvation. But it's also a joyful occasion because of the salvation which Christ won for us by his death and resurrection, and because this meal anticipates the great feast that awaits us in heaven.

4. Prayer

Churches should pray together, both in public worship and at other times. The saying of an 'amen' at the end of your church's prayers may seem like a simple thing, but by it you demonstrate that you are an active participant in your church's worship services rather than a spectator. The person leading at the front is praying on your behalf. Many churches also have regular prayer meetings, and committing yourself to attend whenever you can will hugely help your spiritual maturity over time. We'll think some more in the next chapter about the significance of prayer in the Christian life.

5. Fellowship

Christians share their lives in many ways. They show hospitality to one another. They meet with each other to study the Bible, and they pray together. They talk together about things that are significant, rather than just about the weather – and I live in Scotland, so there's a lot of weather to talk about! They share the struggles of daily life, and encourage one another. As Christians we should be deliberate about building relationships with our brothers and sisters. This is our family, and this is what it means to live a shared life.

6. Service

A final important element in the life of a local church is that we are called to care for one another deeply and serve one another practically. Christians should be known in their communities as people who are a blessing to others. We work together as God's people to serve those around us, and so make known the love of Christ to a world which may be more ready to see it demonstrated than to hear it declared. When a member of your church is in need, others should mobilise to meet that need. There are many ways to encourage that. Our church is organised into 'Care Groups' whose members are all asked to accept a responsibility to care for the others in their group. That might mean visiting someone to read the Scriptures and pray with them during a hard time. It might mean noticing that they haven't been in church for a couple of weeks. It might mean doing their shopping or mowing their lawn.

It is also worth remembering that, unless you're part of a megachurch with a huge staff, church services can only happen because an army of volunteers mobilises each week to serve in all kinds of ways. On a Sunday in our church we have people setting up beforehand (moving chairs, arranging tables), others organising the audio-visual side, some preparing for the music ministry, some on welcome duty, some on crèche or the kids' programme or the teenagers' work, some serving refreshments after the services, and much more. Often these simple, unspectacular areas of service are one of the ways we can bless our church family.

These six areas of church life, are by no means an exhaustive description of what the church does, but these areas are central to the life of the local church. As a new Christian, take time to consider both how you can be nurtured in your faith through them, and how you can support your church in its various ministries. Christians who are committed to serve others in local church fellowships are an enormous blessing to God's people.

A mundane and miraculous mission

Stepping back for a broader view, what we see being played out in God's church is a mundane and miraculous mission.

In one sense, it's mundane. We meet Sunday by Sunday, our Bible studies go on, the church building gets cleaned, the bills get paid, the boiler breaks down… There's a great deal about the life of a local church which is very ordinary.

But we need to recognise that it is, in another sense, miraculous. In local churches around the world, God is giving life to those who are spiritually dead; and he's giving growth to those who have been spiritually dormant; and the Holy Spirit of the God of glory is working powerfully to create a people for himself. In and through the mundane, the miraculous is being played out.

What is also being played out is the mission of God. The church does not exist simply for its own sake. When Jesus left this world to return to the Father, how did he make sure that the earth would be reached with the message of his grace? He established his church. He gave to his people the mission of reaching the world, calling others to repentance and faith, and incorporating them into the fellowship. That means that, while parts of what we do will only ever make sense to Christians, we should welcome unbelievers into our churches as warmly as we can and make it as easy as possible for them to discover who Christ is. It's also important, for the sake of the outsider, that the sense of community I described earlier should be tangible in our churches. If it is, what a glorious advert it is to our community-starved world that the gospel really does work. In Christian termi-nology, an 'apologetic' is a defence of the gospel. Many years ago, Francis Schaeffer argued that the love Christians have for one another is 'the final apologetic'. The ultimate demonstration of the reality of the gospel is the display of the gospel made real in a community.

But more than all of that, the fact that the church is God's mission to the world means that we need to be thoroughly outward-looking in our thinking and living. A warm welcome on a Sunday is not enough, because there are millions who will not come to a Sunday service. That means that we need to take the gospel to them where they are. This is such an important part of the Christian's calling that we'll return to it in Chapter 11.

The church is the location of a mundane and miraculous mission, because in his wisdom God has given to his church an extraordinary place in history. Take a step back. Draw the camera back, out and away from the local church and back far enough to see all God's people throughout the world, and even those who have gone before us and those who will come after us. If you can begin to imagine all Christians throughout time and space, this is the church of Jesus Christ. God has revealed in his word that, however much the world might mock this notion, the church is quite simply what he is doing in history. As Paul puts it, we are all being 'built together into a dwelling place for God by the Spirit' (Ephesians 2:22). Consider these great words of the Scottish preacher Eric Alexander:

> The most significant thing happening in history is the calling, redeeming, and perfecting of the people of God. God is building the church of Jesus Christ. The rest of history is simply a stage God erects for that purpose. He is calling out a people. He is perfecting them. He is changing them...There will come a day, when God will pull down the scaffolding of world history. Do you know what he will be pointing to when he says to the whole creation, 'There is my masterpiece'? He will be pointing to the church of Jesus Christ.[1]

The church could not be more important to every believer. We're in it together. We're in it forever.

---

[1] Eric Alexander, 'The Application of Redemption', in *To Glorify and Enjoy God: A Commemoration of the 350th Anniversary of the Westminster Assembly*, ed. John L. Carson and David W. Hall (Edinburgh: Banner of Truth Trust, 1994), p. 245.

CHAPTER FOUR

Following Jesus in Conversation: The Essentials of Prayer

Do not be anxious about anything, but in everything by prayer and supplication with thanksgiving let your requests be made known to God. – Philippians 4:6.

Introduction: prayer is easy… and hard!

Prayer is the easiest thing in the world. What could be easier than talking to God? It's as easy as a child talking to his or her parent. You need no qualifications, experience or special vocabulary. Prayer is the easiest thing in the world.

Prayer is also the hardest thing in the world. I wonder what proportion of Christians could honestly say that they have a prayer life which is living, disciplined, regular and vibrant. I wonder how many of us could say that we don't struggle with prayer.

It may seem discouraging, in a book on the Christian life, to begin a chapter on prayer by pointing out how difficult it is. But I want to be realistic about the fight that you will face in giving prayer the place that it should have in your life, and to take from prayer the blessing that God has designed it to give you. This is why I want to begin by recognising that, scattered throughout the New Testament, there are all sorts of hints that we might not be alone in finding prayer hard. In a paradoxical way I find it encouraging.

Simply understanding why it seems like such a struggle is a very good thing, but more positively we'll also discover along the way why prayer is so good, precious and worthwhile.

1. Paul found prayer hard

It's clear from his letters that Paul found prayer hard. I don't know why I tend to imagine that it would have been easy for him, but for some reason I don't picture him starting to pray and then immediately remembering that the bins needed to go out. Instead I envisage him soaring in eloquent prayer six times a day, for three hours each time, and revelling in the presence of God. His letters make clear that he did have a strong and disciplined prayer life, but they also make clear that there was nothing easy about it.

Consider how he phrased it when he wrote to the Christians in Rome: 'I appeal to you, brothers, by our Lord Jesus Christ and by the love of the Spirit, to strive together with me in your prayers to God on my behalf...' (Romans 15:30). Paul experiences prayer as a striving, or a struggling, and this is what he invites other Christians to share in. In Colossians also, having written about his struggles and suffering on behalf of the church, he goes on to use that language in a particular way:

> For I want you to know how great a struggle I have for you and for those at Laodicea and for all who have not seen me face to face, that their hearts may be encouraged, being knit together in love, to reach all the riches of full assurance and understanding... (Colossians 2:1-2).

The context makes clear that the 'struggle' Paul is talking about is prayer.

In both of these examples, the word that Paul uses to describe this 'struggle' is the Greek word *agonia*. He agonised in prayer. This is a word you would use to describe someone labouring until they were utterly weary, or a marathon runner nearing the end of the race, or even a soldier battling for his life. Most revealing of all is the other occasion when this word is used in the Scriptures in connection with prayer. Jesus is on his knees, in a garden: 'And being *in an agony* he prayed more earnestly; and his sweat became like great drops of blood falling down to the ground' (Luke 22:44; my emphasis).

Paul's prayers on behalf of others reflect something of that intensity. These verses suggest that it would be a mistake to approach prayer expecting it to be a light and easy thing. We need to prepare ourselves for battle.

2. Paul's colleagues found prayer hard

If there are indications that Paul found prayer hard, there are also indications that his colleagues in ministry had the same experience. Later in Colossians he writes: 'Epaphras, who is one of you, a servant of Christ Jesus, greets you, always struggling on your behalf in his prayers, that you may stand mature and fully assured in all the will of God' (Colossians 4:12). The word 'struggle' reminds us of Jacob 'wrestling' with the angel in order to gain the blessing (Gen. 23:24-28). Praying for blessing was a hard struggle for both Jacob and Epaphras.

3. Paul's readers found prayer hard

Finally, it seems that Paul's readers also found prayer hard. We can assume that from the fact that he is constantly urging them, encouraging them and pleading with them to pray. Again, Colossians provides an example: 'Continue steadfastly in prayer, being watchful in it with thanksgiving' (Colossians 4:2). 'Continue steadfastly' is a single word in the original Greek: literally Paul tells us to 'be strong in the direction of prayer'. Press on towards it with urgency and intensity, and persevere until your goal is reached.

Surely we all know that prayer is important, so why does Paul so often remind Christians to pray? Because he knows that they will be tempted not to. Because he knows that prayer is hard. Jesus knew it too, which is why he told his disciples a parable about a persistent widow, to show them 'that they ought always to pray and not lose heart' (Luke 18:1). He knew that his people would quickly become disheartened in prayer, and would want to give up. Jesus himself knew that prayer is hard.

That, in the end, is the greatest comfort of all – the knowledge that 'we do not have a high priest who is unable to sympathise with our weaknesses, but one who in every respect has been tempted as we are, yet without sin' (Hebrews 4:15). He knows. He understands. And he stands ready to help.

So far we've only really established that prayer is hard, and no-one's going to get a Ph.D. just for realising that. It might be encouraging to know that it's not just me, but that doesn't really change anything. So let's see if we can edge towards some practical help by asking *why* prayer is so hard.

Prayer is hard because the sinful, selfish heart does not want to pray

The first reason prayer is hard is that the sinful, selfish heart does not want to pray. That is not what I want to say at this point. I want to say that prayer is hard because modern life is so busy. There are so many distractions nowadays, and so many demands on my time. If Paul had only known about the school run, and the demands of the modern workplace, and how much time it takes to keep Facebook updated, he would have been more realistic in his expectations.

Circumstances can certainly make habits of prayer easier or harder, but we've already seen that the difficulty of prayer is not a phenomenon of modern life. It has always been this way, because the difficulty of prayer is a consequence of fallen human nature. In the beginning, God walked with Adam and Eve in the garden in the cool of the day (Genesis 3:8), and they must have spoken with him freely and joyfully. Once sin entered the world, however, 'the man and his wife hid themselves from the presence of the LORD God among the trees of the garden'. Apart from the foolishness of trying to hide from God, sense the tragedy of it: suddenly, speaking to God has become difficult. The difficulty is part of the disruption to the relationship, because the heart of man has turned away from God.

This is the ugly fact we have to face. The basic reason why prayer is hard is because the sinful, selfish heart does not want to pray. Prayer is in no sense technically difficult. It's the easiest thing in the world: you just talk to God. The difficult thing is not the *doing* of it, but the *desiring* of it. In our fallen nature we do not have within us the desire that we should have for fellowship with the living God. This is the fundamental problem, and the reason why prayerlessness cannot be tackled as an isolated issue, unrelated to the rest of our Christian lives. To find prayer hard is normal, but to give up on prayer indicates a deep spiritual problem. There needs to be change at the level of the heart, coming from a deepening understanding of the gospel and a growing desire for fellowship with God in Christ.

Prayer is hard because it is central to our growth in grace

That takes us to a second stage in our thinking. Prayer is hard because it is central to our growth in grace. Prayer is hard in the same sense that faith is hard when we want to walk by sight, and obedience is hard when we want to do our own thing, and love for Christ is hard when we want to love ourselves. Prayer is part of the lifelong process whereby God weans us from the silliness and selfishness in which we live by our own fallen nature, and introduces us to the life of grace and glory.

Prayer is a core part of our discipleship, and a central element in relationship with God. Prayer involves the expression of praise and thankfulness, and the confession of sin, all wrapped up in trust and dependence. In all these ways it is intimately connected with every aspect of the Christian life. So, since the Christian life is hard, prayer is hard.

Furthermore, prayer is a central element in our sanctification. The clue is in the fact that prayer has been given to us with a feature which can best be illustrated by reference to the movies. I am reliably informed (by Hollywood) that police-issue handguns and semi-automatic weapons come with a safety catch. I would guess – and hope – that nuclear weapons have multiple fail-safe devices, so that you can't set them off by accident either. The principle is that things with the potential to unleash great power tend to have a safety catch. Prayer wields the power of God. There is no weapon more powerful than this, so all true prayer has a built-in safety catch. When Jesus taught his people to pray during the Sermon on the Mount, part of the pattern he gave them to follow was that all their prayers should be wrapped up in one all-encompassing prayer: 'Your will be done' (Matthew 6:10). This is prayer's essential safety catch. We are neither good enough nor wise enough to know perfectly what we should be praying for, so we qualify all of our praying in this way: Lord, do this, but only if it's in line with your will and purpose.

This reflects a deeply important prayer principle which is often overlooked, namely that prayer is not about bending God's will to ours but about bending our will to his. The value of prayer, as Michael Wilcock puts it, 'lies not in getting the Lord to do what I want, but in learning to want what the Lord is going to do'.[1] In that process of leaving behind the old life and embracing the new, prayer plays a central role. Through it, God moulds our hearts to reflect the likeness of his more and more.

That helps, again, to explain why prayer is so hard. This is the instrument that God uses to do really penetrating soul-work within us. We cannot pray 'Thy Kingdom come, thy will be done' as Christ teaches us, and keep our own agenda directing our lives. We cannot pray 'Give us this day our daily bread', and retain the sense of self-sufficiency and autonomy that we so love. We cannot pray 'Forgive us our sins', and continue in cherished wrongdoing that we're not really determined to stamp out. We cannot add 'as we forgive those who have sinned against us', and hang on to grudges against others.

[1] Michael Wilcock, *The Message of Psalms 1-72* (Leicester: IVP, 2001), p. 137.

At every stage, prayer forces us to put self to death and give God his rightful place on the throne of our lives. It is not easy to keep the safety catch on prayer, always submitting our desires to God's purposes. It's one thing if I'm praying for a dry day for the church barbecue, but what if my prayer is, 'Lord, make my cancer treatment effective'? How hard is it then to add the words 'but your will be done'? That's tough, but God will allow us to hold nothing back from his sovereignty. His call to trust encompasses the whole of life. Prayer is one of the central ways in which he drives that home to us, and makes it real in us, which is surely one of the reasons why prayer is so hard. It's also one of the reasons why Jesus agonised in prayer there in Gethsemane, because in his human nature he longed to avoid the death that lay before him. And yet, even then, what was his prayer? 'Father, if you are willing, remove this cup from me. Nevertheless, not my will, but yours, be done' (Luke 22:42).

Prayer is hard because it is powerful and effective to change the world

Encouragingly, another reason why prayer is so hard is that it is powerful and effective to change the world. The Scriptures are very clear about the power of prayer. In 1 Kings 17-18, Elijah declared that the heavens would close, and, resultantly, there was no rain for three and a half years. What kind of a man was this? James gives us the answer: 'Elijah was a man with a nature like ours' (James 5:17). He was just like you and me. Nonetheless, through believing prayer he harnessed the power of God. God has invested prayer with an extraordinary power. He remains free and sovereign, and in no sense do our prayers control him, but we can feel the truth and force of the comment that David Dickson made, back in the nineteenth century, when he wrote his classic book, *The Elder and His Work*: 'Prayer is the most practical and powerful thing in the world, for it moves the Hand that moves the universe.'[2]

[2] David Dickson, *The Elder and his Work*, ed. George Kennedy McFarland and Philip Graham Ryken (Phillipsburg: Presbyterian & Reformed, 2004), p. 80.

That is immensely exciting work to be involved in, but is it work that you would expect to be easy and relaxing? If prayer is this powerful and effective, and if it gives us a meaningful role in the very workings of God, we should expect that it is going to be hard work. The power at work belongs to God, not us, but to be involved in any way in the exercise of it is not something that we should expect to be able to take lightly. The Prime Minister or President doesn't have a diary with entries like: 'Signed some letters... launched nuclear warheads... had a sandwich.' The unleashing of great power is a solemn and weighty thing, and prayer is powerful and effective to change the world.

Prayer is hard because Satan hates and fears prayer

Given the way in which prayer reshapes us and reshapes the world in line with the will and purpose of God, we need to recognise another of the reasons that prayer is hard is that Satan hates and fears prayer. This is a focal-point of spiritual warfare: we fight the fight of faith on the battleground of prayer.

Tim Keller tells the story of Æthelfrith, who was a Saxon king of Northumbria and a pagan. He had invaded Wales, and was about to give battle. The Welsh armies were arrayed against him, but he noticed one group of unarmed men over to the side. Asking who they were, he was told that they were the Christian monks of Bangor, set there to pray for the success of their army. Æthelfrith may have been a pagan, but this was his response: 'Attack them *first*.'[3]

Imagine this. Satan steps on to the battlefield of your life. Your forces are mustered before him. He sees a battalion representing your determination that you will be faithful to God and resist Satan. He does not fear that. Next to that is a battalion of your past achievements. He doesn't fear that. Further over is a battalion of your spiritual wisdom. He doesn't fear that. His eye turns to a

---

[3] Timothy Keller, *Prayer: Experiencing Awe and Intimacy with God* (London: Hodder & Stoughton, 2014), p. 225.

battalion of your moral upbringing. He doesn't fear that. He turns to consider a battalion representing your knowledge of the gospel. He doesn't even turn back at that. But then he spots a battalion representing the prayer which will breathe life into everything else, and channel the power of God through everything else. Now, where will he attack?

The reason prayer is such a struggle so often for so many Christians, is because this is where the battle is won or lost. Nothing else counts for anything if we are not praying, because 'Unless the LORD builds the house, those who build it labour in vain' (Psalm 127:1). Satan knows this, and so he often attacks Christians at this point. Samuel Chadwick, a Methodist minister in the late nineteenth- and early twentieth-century, wrote:

> Satan dreads nothing but prayer. His one concern is to keep the saints from praying. He fears nothing from prayerless studies, prayerless work, prayerless religion. He laughs at our toil, mocks our wisdom, but trembles when we pray.[4]

This is why so many other things get in the way when we try to pray, and why our minds are so prone to wander. This is why the phone rings, or the doorbell goes, or we suddenly wonder if we left the iron on in the other room, or we remember about a quick e-mail that we need to send before we forget. Prayer is hard because this is spiritual warfare, and our opponent plays dirty.

Prayer is hard because prayer is precious

But all of these things should encourage us to realise how absolutely worthwhile the struggle – even the agony – is. You can summarise it like this: prayer is hard because it's precious. This just seems to be a law of life: all that is most precious is the most difficult. God uses prayer as one of his most powerful tools in the shaping of his people, moulding our sinful, selfish hearts into obedient, loving ones. God uses prayer as one of his most powerful weapons to change the

---

[4] Quoted in J. Oswald Sanders, *Effective Prayer* (Singapore: OMF, 1961), p. 7.

world, seeing his kingdom come and his will done. God uses prayer to frustrate the efforts of the evil one, bringing about what is good, true and right. This is the precious work that we're invited to be a part of, just by talking to our God – the simplest thing in the world.

Prayer: good news for the battling Christian

The good news is that God knows that this simple thing is very hard, and he promises to help us as we pray. Consider two passages of Scripture which encourage us in that.

The first is a simple expression from Ephesians 6. Paul describes the different parts of the armour of God which will equip us for the Christian life, and then he adds that we are to put them all on, 'praying at all times in the Spirit, with all prayer and supplication' (verse 18). What does it mean to pray 'in the Spirit'? It means that God helps us to pray, so that we do so by the power of his Holy Spirit; and it means that God guides us in prayer, leading us by his Spirit so that we increasingly pray in line with his will. So this is not just a command that we pray, but a promise that God himself will aid us as we do. As he helps us in everything else, he will help us in prayer.

The second passage, which is of great comfort to God's people, is Romans 8. We've been given the Spirit of adoption as sons, by whom we cry, 'Abba! Father!' (verse 15). But Paul knows that there will still be times when we struggle in prayer, or when we genuinely don't know what to pray, or when we struggle to verbalise our prayers, or when we cry out to God about things that are so dear to us that our emotions overwhelm us. And so:

> the Spirit helps us in our weakness. For we do not know what to pray for as we ought, but the Spirit himself intercedes for us with groanings too deep for words. And he who searches hearts knows what is the mind of the Spirit, because the Spirit intercedes for the saints according to the will of God (Romans 8:26-27).

God's Spirit, searching your heart, knows your deepest desires for the glory of God in his world and the work of God in your life. That means that God does not refuse to hear or respond to our prayers because we failed to articulate ourselves very clearly. When our praying fails, as it sometimes does, he takes it up and completes it. This is how gracious God is: we are so helpless that we need help in the very act of seeking help – but this is what he gives us.

Precious principles for prayer

It will be of great practical help to your prayer life if you remember two precious principles for prayer.

First, prayer is not a burden but *a gift*. It is not primarily something God demands of us, but something God gives to us. It is an expression of his grace towards us, allowing us to engage in meaningful relationship with him each day, and inviting us to bring our needs to him.

Secondly, as we saw above, prayer is not about getting what we want, but about *seeking what God wants*. Imagine the alternative. Can you picture what would happen if God had so designed things that our prayers were automatically granted all of the time, so that everything we asked for we were given? Can you imagine the chaos that would be unleashed in the world by all of our competing demands, and our ignorant requests, and our selfish requirements? Someone is supposed to have said once that if God had answered every prayer he had ever asked, he would have been married to nine different women! It's a good point.

Because of our sinfulness and our smallness, there will be many times when our prayers are faulty. There will be times when we ask God for things that seem good to us but which, if we knew everything that God knows, we would never have asked for in the first place. That doesn't mean we shouldn't ask for things in prayer, because we are commanded to do so, but our aim should always be to pray in line with the purposes of God as he has revealed them to us in his word. Also, we need to keep the safety catch on, qualifying our prayers in recognition of our weakness and sinfulness. We speak to God on the basis of the light that he has given us, but we acknowledge that we don't have all the facts and we don't have perfect wisdom, and ultimately we want God to do what he knows to be good and right. As we ask, we recognise the whole time that God may often have to say 'no'. Faith is humble enough to accept God's 'no'.

Practical priorities in prayer

If you've never really prayed before, where do you begin? Well, prayer is something that we learn to do and Jesus is our best teacher. Like the disciples of old, we ask him to teach us to pray. A healthy prayer life will not stand alone in our lives, while the rest of our spiritual life withers, but will walk hand-in-hand with the general condition of our relationship with Christ. That means that it's connected to our Bible reading, our church attendance, our fellowship with other Christians, and so on.

First, I want to encourage you to *make prayer a priority in your daily life*. Make it part of the regular rhythm of your day. Find a time and a place that works for you. It's usually helpful to tie our prayer in with our regular Bible reading, as the word of God will prompt us to pray in response to God's goodness. Don't worry if your first attempts at prayer are intermittent and stumbling and short. When a toddler begins to walk, his parents aren't appalled by how unsteady he is on his feet. The tiniest step delights them. Likewise, God is not waiting to pounce on hesitation or uncertainty in your praying. Remember that you are coming to a perfect Father who loves you.

I would also encourage you to spend some time studying the Lord's Prayer. In Luke 11, Jesus' disciples asked him, 'Lord, teach us to pray…' His response was to provide them with a prayer which is really a pattern for prayer. Matthew 6:9-13 includes a slightly expanded version. It's worth memorising this, as many churches ask everyone to say it together in Sunday services. The most common form used in churches is:

Our Father, who art in heaven, hallowed be thy name. Thy kingdom come, thy will be done on earth as it is in heaven. Give us this day our daily bread, and forgive us our debts [or *trespasses*] as we forgive our debtors [or *those who trespass against us*]. And lead us not into temptation, but deliver us from evil. For thine is the kingdom, the power and the glory for ever, amen.

Through this prayer, Jesus teaches us to praise God and to seek his honour, to ask that his will be done in the world, to acknowledge our dependence on him for everything, to seek forgiveness for sin, and to take seriously our obligation to forgive others, to seek his protection in trials and temptations, and to recognise that all glory belongs to him. Using the Lord's Prayer is good, but don't just recite it as a formula. Rather, consider the shape and themes of it, to help you to think about how you yourself might pray.

Related to this, you could do worse than to follow an old pattern for prayer using the acronym A.C.T.S. The *A* stands for *adoration*, reminding us that prayer is not merely about asking God for things but about expressing our love for him and our wonder at his greatness. Often our Bible reading will prompt us to adore some particular aspect of God's character. *C* stands for *confession*, reminding us that we are sinners approaching a holy God. We need to keep short accounts with him, confessing our sins freely and often. *T* stands for *thanksgiving*, reminding us that every good thing we have comes from God's gracious hand and this should be acknowledged. *S* stands for *supplication*, inviting us to bring our requests to the God who loves us and gives generously to us.

If you're married, pray with your husband or wife. Christian husbands have a particular responsibility to lead their wives in this. If you have children, make family prayers a normal part of your life, and train your children to pray regularly and meaningfully. Saying grace before meals is also a helpful practice since it builds prayer into everyday life, as well as reminding us several times a day that every good thing we have is a gift from God. Prayer therefore encourages an attitude of perpetual thankfulness to God.

Christians sometimes contrast regular dedicated times of prayer with an approach to prayer reminding us several times a day that every good thing we have is God's gift to us. Prayer therefore encourages. This encourages us to live in the awareness of God's presence and care, and to make our faith real in all that we're saying and thinking and doing. The great thing is that we don't have to choose. Both of these approaches to prayer are immensely helpful, so why not harness the power of both?

Secondly, I want to encourage you to *participate actively in the prayers of your church Sunday by Sunday.* I don't mean that you should barge up to the front and demand to lead, but that you should listen carefully to what is being prayed. Engage meaningfully with your church's prayers, making them your own, so that you can say a hearty 'amen' to them. By doing this you are praying, with your family, to your Father.

Thirdly, I want to encourage you to *learn to pray out loud with other Christians.* I know that some believers find this very intimidating, but the best approach is to throw yourself into it as soon as you can. It may be that you can meet up with another Christian or two and support one another in prayer. It may be that you can pray with others in a small group Bible study. It may be that your church has a regular prayer meeting, in which case I would strongly encourage you to support it wherever possible. God has told us that he chooses to act in response to the prayers of his people. On that basis I have a deep conviction that, in general, the health of the church tomorrow can be measured by the health of the prayer meeting today. The church I serve meets every Thursday evening for prayer, as well as every Sunday morning. It's nothing spectacular. In fact, it often strikes me that by any worldly standard there could be nothing more pathetic than huddles of Christians with their heads bowed, muttering into the air. Yet this is where the work of God is done. This is where warriors step on to the field. This is where kingdom battles are fought and won.

Vitus Theodorus was a German theologian and a friend of the great Reformer Martin Luther. He once said: 'I overheard him in prayer… with what life and spirit did he pray! It was with so much reverence, as if he were speaking to God, yet with so much confidence as if he were speaking to his friend.'[5]

It is an immense privilege to be able to speak to the living God as if to a friend. May we use it well.

---

[5] Quoted by C. H. Spurgeon, *Lectures to My Students* (Edinburgh: Banner of Truth Trust, 2008), pp. 47-48.

CHAPTER FIVE

Following Jesus by His Power:
The Essentials of the Holy Spirit

I have said all these things to you to keep you from falling away.
² They will put you out of the synagogues. Indeed, the hour is coming
when whoever kills you will think he is offering service to God.
³ And they will do these things because they have not known the
Father, nor me. ⁴ But I have said these things to you, that when
their hour comes you may remember that I told them to you.

I did not say these things to you from the beginning, because
I was with you. ⁵ But now I am going to him who sent me, and
none of you asks me, 'Where are you going?' ⁶ But because I have
said these things to you, sorrow has filled your heart. ⁷ Nevertheless,
I tell you the truth: it is to your advantage that I go away, for if I
do not go away, the Helper will not come to you. But if I go, I will
send him to you. ⁸ And when he comes, he will convict the world
concerning sin and righteousness and judgement: ⁹ concerning
sin, because they do not believe in me; ¹⁰ concerning righteousness,
because I go to the Father, and you will see me no longer;
¹¹ concerning judgement, because the ruler of this world is judged.
¹² I still have many things to say to you, but you cannot bear them
now. ¹³ When the Spirit of truth comes, he will guide you into all
the truth, for he will not speak on his own authority, but whatever
he hears he will speak, and he will declare to you the things that are
to come. ¹⁴ He will glorify me, for he will take what is mine and
declare it to you. ¹⁵ All that the Father has is mine; therefore I said
that he will take what is mine and declare it to you. – John 16:1-15.

Introduction: Father, Son and...?

We have a problem, and it's a big one. Our greatest need in life is to be in relationship with God, but we're a million miles from him. He is powerful beyond the wildest stretches of our imagination, and we are weak and limited. He is everywhere, and we are very small. He is infinitely wise, and we are so limited in our knowledge and understanding. More significantly yet, he is utterly perfect in holiness, and we are sinners, and most seriously of all, we are in ourselves spiritually dead. By our fallen nature we have no desire for God, and so are unable and unwilling to resolve the problem of our sinfulness before him. What's more, even if God acts to do so and holds salvation out to us, in ourselves we are unable and unwilling even to receive it. In the normal course of things, we would all be headed for an eternity separated from God and from all goodness, with absolutely nothing we could do to change that fact. None of this is pleasant to consider, but if we're ever to grasp how glorious and gracious the gospel really is, we need to go through the unpleasantness of realising how appalling our condition is apart from Christ. This is what the Bible teaches. This is God's verdict on the human condition.

Given all of that, how can there be any hope? How could I ever be restored to this God, who loves me so dearly, and who longs for me to know eternal joy, but whom *I don't want*? Even if he is gracious towards me, and extends a love and a forgiveness to me which is utterly undeserved, how can I ever receive it when I am not interested in it? In any case, how could I ever live to please such a holy God? How is it possible for me to know God as a living presence in my life?

The answer to all of these questions is: the Holy Spirit. That's this chapter in a nutshell: the reason we can have a living relationship with God is because of the Holy Spirit. The Spirit's work in our lives is therefore crucial, and yet many Christians live with only the vaguest (and sometimes, let's be honest, the strangest) notions about who or what this 'Holy Spirit' is. Fortunately our salvation doesn't depend on understanding God. If it did, we'd all be in trouble! Nonetheless, our joy, confidence and fruitfulness as believers will increase if we come to understand who the Holy Spirit is and what he does in our lives.

Let's begin with the most basic truth of all: the Holy Spirit is God. We're not talking here about some kind of impersonal power, like an esoteric Eastern religion or 'the Force' from *Star Wars*. The Holy Spirit is not some kind of strange ghostly presence (despite often having been referred to in the past as 'the Holy Ghost'). To understand this more clearly, we need to grasp how the Bible's understanding of the nature of God is completely unique in the whole of history. It tells us that God always was, and is today, and always will be, triune – the Trinity. He is God the Father, and God the Son, and God the Holy Spirit. Father, Son and Spirit are all God. They are not each one third of God, but they are each all of God. They are not God appearing in different forms at different times, as if he changes from one to the other. The Bible clearly portrays them as distinct persons, but persons who share one nature. They work together, in perfect harmony, in every crucial aspect of our salvation. Father, Son and Spirit are so closely interwoven that the Bible sometimes refers to the Holy Spirit as 'the Spirit of Jesus'; and Jesus in Matthew 10:20 refers to 'the Spirit of your Father'. There is a unique work granted to each, which is why we can have a chapter about the distinctive work of the Holy Spirit in your life, but we should remember that the Father, Son and Spirit never work separately from one another.

Historically, the church has affirmed the doctrine of the Trinity by saying that there are three persons in one God. You take the prefix tri- (as in triangle or tripod), and you add the word unity, and you get the word Trinity (Three-in-One). In the end this is a deep mystery, and there's no unravelling it. There is no analogy that works. God is not like a shamrock, with three leaves. He is not like H2O, existing as water and ice and steam. These analogies don't work, because he is just not like anything else. In fact, when God revealed himself to Moses long ago, and Moses asked what his name was, he said, 'I am who I am' (Exodus 3:14). In other words, God cannot be defined or described by reference to anything else. He is who he is, and as the Bible unfolds he reveals that *who he is* is God the Father, God the Son and God the Spirit – one God. (Since the Holy Spirit is God, by the way, we refer to him as 'him' and not 'it'. He is a person. How would you like being called 'it'?)

The Holy Spirit's one great passion and goal

Our aim in this chapter is to grasp the basics of the work which the Holy Spirit does in the world as a whole, in the church, and in your life. I hope you'll be thrilled by it. Before we launch into these three areas, though, we need to establish the most important thing of all. Everything else hangs on this, and if you take only one thing from this chapter, take this: *the Holy Spirit has one great passion and goal, which is to glorify Jesus Christ by bringing men and women to worship, love, trust and obey him.* Take the time to read that sentence again, and absorb it. It could save you a great deal of confusion and grief in your Christian life.

You may be aware by now that different churches understand the work of the Holy Spirit differently. Charismatic and Pentecostal churches place emphasis on a particular experience of the Spirit, and on certain spiritual gifts, but I would encourage you to be very careful about the assumption that the Spirit works today in exactly the same ways he did in the New Testament era. By definition that was a unique period, and there are very good reasons to believe that God gave special gifts to his church to authenticate the message of the gospel as it was taking hold in the world for the first time. I would also encourage you to be very careful about the assumption that the work of the Holy Spirit can be measured by intense emotional experiences.

Although I believe that certain specific supernatural gifts of the Spirit (such as prophecy and apostleship) ceased at the end of the New Testament era, that doesn't mean that the Holy Spirit is less active or has less of a role to play in our Christian lives. But the biblical emphasis is different, and leads us in different directions. Crucially, the Holy Spirit doesn't want our focus to be on him. J. I. Packer describes how the Spirit acts as a kind of spotlight, directing our attention to Christ himself:

> When floodlighting is well done, the floodlights are so placed that you do not see them; you are not in fact supposed to see where the light is coming from; what you are meant to see is just the building on which the floodlights are trained… The Spirit's message is never, 'Look at me; listen to me; come to me; get to know me,' but always, 'Look at *him*, and see his glory; listen to *him*, and hear his word; go to *him*, and have his life; get to know *him*, and taste *his* gift of joy and peace.'[1]

This means that the true sign of the presence of God's Spirit among his people is not that you can feel or sense him, or that obviously spectacular things are happening. The way you really know that the Spirit is present and at work is this: where Christ is being exalted, where he is being seen for who he is, where the grace of his gospel is being communicated with clarity and power, where his call to repentance, faith and renewal is being heard and heeded, where men and women are being transformed into his image, where they're being shaped into a radical new community of mutual submission and service, and where through all of this God is being glorified through Christ – there you have clear evidence of the presence and power of the Holy Spirit.

---

[1] J. I. Packer, *Keeping in Step with the Spirit: Finding Fullness in Our Walk with God* (Grand Rapids: Baker, 2005), p. 57, emphasis original.

The Holy Spirit at work in history

The Bible makes clear that the Holy Spirit has been active through-out history. He was there in the beginning, at the creation of the universe. We read in Genesis 1:2 that: 'The earth was without form and void, and darkness was over the face of the deep. And the Spirit of God was hovering over the face of the waters.' Since we learn from John 1:1-3 that the Son of God (referred to there as 'the Word') was also there, and that everything was made through him, we know that Father and Son and Spirit were all involved in the work of crea-tion.

The Holy Spirit can be seen at work throughout Old Testament history, bringing about the purposes of God. When God wants to speak to his people, he appoints prophets and speaks through them by his Holy Spirit. The Spirit works in them to ensure that what they say is the message that God wants to be delivered.

Similarly, when God decides to make himself known to us through the Scriptures, how does that happen? We saw in Chapter 2 that 'no prophecy was ever produced by the will of man, but men spoke from God as they were carried along by the Holy Spirit' (2 Peter 1:21).

At various points throughout Old Testament history, the Holy Spirit also descends upon people in a particularly powerful way, to enable them to perform a specific task. For example, when Israel's first king (Saul) rebelled against God, and God appointed David to replace him, we read that 'the Spirit of the LORD rushed upon David from that day forward' but that 'the Spirit of the LORD departed from Saul' (1 Samuel 16:13-14). Israel's king had a special role to perform in the purpose of God, and needed a special presence and empowering of God to do it.

Also, throughout history, it is the Holy Spirit who gives the gift of faith to God's people. He enables them to trust in the Saviour whom God promises to send. He gives them assurance of salvation, and he gives them power to live for God. That doesn't make God's people perfect by any means; the same David surrendered to sexual temptation, had an affair with Bathsheba, and was drawn into murder. But what was his prayer after he realised the seriousness of what he'd done? 'Cast me not away from your presence, and take not your Holy Spirit from me. Restore to me the joy of your salvation…' (Psalm 51:11-12).

In all these ways and more, the Holy Spirit is constantly active and working in Old Testament history. In particular, he is constantly preparing the way for Jesus to come. Remember that his first priority and passion is to see Jesus glorified. To that end the Spirit descended in fullest measure upon Jesus himself, and in time was actively and powerfully involved in the establishing of the church and in the giving of the New Testament, right up to the point where the Bible was completed.

The Holy Spirit at work in the church

Secondly, we need to recognise that the Holy Spirit is at work in the church. He builds the church, gives unity between true believers, and gives gifts to God's people. If you're a disciple of Jesus, then not only do you have the Holy Spirit in your life, but you have a unique set of gifts which he has given to you. Some of these are natural gifts which were part of your personality before you became a Christian, but which have now been increased and harnessed in the service of Christ. Others may be special gifts which the Holy Spirit gives to you which go far beyond anything you would naturally have known. In any case these are things which he has given to you, not just for your own sake, but for the sake of the church as a whole.

You may hear a lot about 'using your gifts', which is important, but even here we need to be careful. God gives gifts to his people for the benefit of his church, but be cautious in guarding your heart. Make sure that your attitude in the church is always one of servant-heartedness, rather than one of being 'entitled' to exercise your gift. The use of gifts can easily degenerate into an exercise in self-promotion, and it has often become a source of contention in the church. Don't fall into that trap. Remember that, whatever else the Bible says about spiritual gifts, one thing is very clear: the main emphasis is that they are gifts of service. Here, too, the key to a healthy Christian life is keeping the main thing the main thing. Spiritual gifts are never about status, but always about service. If you ever find yourself feeling that you have the 'right' to use your gifts and demanding to do so, this is a danger sign. We need to constantly remind ourselves that gifts are given to us, not for our own gratification, but so that we might be a blessing to the church family. Vaughan Roberts puts it like this:

> Some Christians seem to be paralysed. Rather than serving others, they are waiting to discover what their gift is. The right question to ask is not so much 'What is my gift?' as 'How can I serve?' As soon as we see a possible area of service that we could fill, we should get moving. And, in so far as God uses that service for the good of the church, we are exercising a spiritual gift.[2]

That's great advice, especially for a young Christian. Ask yourself the question: how can I serve my brothers and sisters in Christ? What could I do that would be a blessing to them? In a healthy church, these questions are being asked all the time, and answered in all sorts of ways: through quiet words of encouragement, through phone calls and visits, through pots of soup delivered to the door, through homes opened in hospitality, through the assurance of prayer for a fellow believer, through every aspect of the shared life of community. None of this is rocket science. In some ways it's just kindness and common sense in the service of the gospel. It's just what it looks like to care for one another as a family. But as we do that, we discover that we're using the gifts that God has given us in joyful service for one another, and that is a beautiful and God-honouring thing. That's the Spirit at work in the church.

[2] Vaughan Roberts, *True Worship* (Carlisle: Authentic, 2002), pp. 76-77.

The Holy Spirit at work in you

However, before any of that can take place in the church as a whole, there's a deeper work that the Holy Spirit needs to perform in your life and mine. To grasp this, it's helpful to read what Jesus told his disciples about the Spirit's work in John 16:1-15. This is part of what we call Jesus' 'Farewell Discourse', which is an extended section of teaching on the night before his crucifixion. Here he explains to his disciples that he must leave them, and to their amazement he insists that it is better for them that he should go away. If you've ever been tempted to think how much easier the Christian life would be if you could have seen Jesus in the flesh, this is the antidote. He himself tells his disciples that it is better that he should go, and that the Holy Spirit should come. Why?

What Jesus knows, and what his disciples have not yet understood, is that he must go to his death and resurrection in order to accomplish our salvation, and he must then send his Holy Spirit to make that salvation real to us. The Holy Spirit comes as the carrier of the gospel. Not only that, but he makes the presence of God and the power of God available to us in a new way. Earlier that same evening, Jesus described the Holy Spirit as 'another Helper, to be with you for ever' who 'dwells with you and will be in you' (John 14:16-17). The Holy Spirit therefore makes God a continual, living presence in our lives. He will dwell with us and be in us, so that we are never alone. This is a soul-steadying truth. God's gift of his Spirit is the gift of his own presence with us, at all times, and through all things.

To give this some shape, let's pick out three aspects of the Spirit's work in the believer.

1. He convicts and converts

First, he convicts and converts. Becoming a believer involves being convicted of sin, in the sense of realising that we are guilty before God. We have disobeyed the God to whom we owe everything, we deserve his condemnation, and we therefore stand in need of a forgiveness to which we have no right. This conviction of sin is the work of the Holy Spirit within us.

If you're a Christian, the reason is not that you finally figured out the meaning of life, or achieved spiritual clarity, or even that you 'made a decision' to trust in Jesus. If you're a Christian today, that is because the Holy Spirit convicted you of your sin before God; and as he did so, amazingly, graciously, he gave you a new heart that allowed you to respond to him. That's why, at some point, you found that you were willing and able to do what you had never been willing and able to do before – to confess your sinfulness before God and to repent of it. A wise friend once said to me of his conversion, 'You know, it *felt so much* like my decision.' He knew that, at a deeper level, it was the grace of God taking hold of him and putting new life in him, by the power of the Spirit. This is the only way anyone ever comes to faith. This is why C. H. Spurgeon, who was one of the greatest preachers in history, used to walk to the pulpit saying to himself, over and over, 'I believe in the Holy Spirit.' No human being, however gifted, can give life to dead sinners. But if the Spirit of God takes the word of God and makes it real to men and women, then everything changes. Suddenly, the Bible comes to life! The cross of Christ opens up to us: *that was for me!* The whole thing comes alive, and we see both that we are great sinners, and that Christ is a great Saviour. It all happens because the Holy Spirit has taken that saving work of Jesus, which was always there, and applied it to our hearts so that it becomes real to us.

When that happens in your life, that is the Holy Spirit at work. From that point 'he dwells with you and will be in you' (John 14:17). Notice what Jesus is saying there: all believers have the Holy Spirit. Don't ever let anyone tell you that you first become a Christian, and there's then a later experience when you 'receive the Holy Spirit'. Jesus – whose Spirit we're talking about – says otherwise.

2. He teaches and trains

A second aspect of the Spirit's work in the believer is that he teaches and trains. 'But the Helper, the Holy Spirit, whom the Father will send in my name, he will teach you all things and bring to your remembrance all that I have said to you' (John 14:26).

There are two stages in the fulfilment of those promises. The Spirit began by guiding the apostles in the writing of the New Testament. He brought to their remembrance what Jesus had taught them, and he guided them into the truth. Once more, 'men spoke from God as they were carried along by the Holy Spirit' (2 Peter 1:21). But a point came when the Scriptures were completed, and this collected body of God's authoritative revelation closed. So today, the way the Holy Spirit teaches and trains us is through the written word of God, which is complete and sufficient. The life of discipleship is not one in which we strain to hear a mystical 'voice of God' telling us what to do this afternoon, but one in which we immerse ourselves in the Scriptures until God's thinking becomes our thinking. As we do that, the Spirit will be our teacher, and will take the truths of God's word and make them real to us. Just as the Spirit inspired the writing of these words, so now he will illuminate our reading. We discover that what God spoke, God speaks. We discover that this word of God is 'living and active, piercing to the division of soul and spirit, of joints and of marrow, and discerning the thoughts and intentions of the heart' (Hebrews 4:12). The Holy Spirit takes the word and applies it to our hearts and lives.

3. He equips and empowers

A final area of the Spirit's work that I want to highlight is that he equips and empowers. At John 14:16 Jesus describes the promised Holy Spirit as 'the Helper'. That word in Greek (the language that the New Testament was originally written in) which is used in several places in this section, is a notoriously difficult one to translate, but it is also a wonderful word. Literally it means 'one who is called alongside'. That could signify a number of things. In secular Greek it was the word for an advocate, who stands with you and defends you in a court of law. (I spent seven years as a court lawyer. I like to flatter myself that my clients were better off with me called alongside them than without me – but, to be fair, you'd have to ask them.) It could also signify standing with someone to strengthen them in times of difficulty, encourage them in times of weariness, counsel them in times of confusion, comfort them in times of pain, or spur forward in times of hesitancy. In all these ways, the Spirit is our Helper. Amazingly, he is *God-called-alongside-us*! This is how God becomes a living presence in your daily life, and how his power becomes available to you so that you can live a life for him that you could never live by your own strength. It's just not possible to live the Christian life except by the power of God working in us, through the Holy Spirit. As we'll see in the next chapter, over time the Spirit comes to shape our character and our living more and more so that certain fruit is produced in our lives: namely love, joy, peace, patience, kindness, goodness, faithfulness, gentleness and self-control (Galatians 5:22-23).

These are the core aspects of the Holy Spirit's work in you: he convicts and converts, he teaches and trains, he equips and empowers.

Conclusion: surrendering to freedom

All of this leads to two practical conclusions. First, we must keep coming back to the word of God, the Bible. This is what the Spirit will use to bring us to maturity, so we need to spend much time in the word, and ask the Spirit to open our eyes more and more fully to its truths, so that we can live more and more completely for the glory of Christ. He will answer that prayer, for his one great passion and goal is to glorify Jesus Christ by bringing men and women to worship, love, trust and obey him.

The Spirit will delight to equip and empower you for the glory of Christ.

The second practical conclusion is this: total surrender. In some Christian circles, being 'filled with the Spirit' is spoken of as if this were something designed primarily to give us amazing experiences. Contrast that with what Oswald Sanders once wrote about Christian leaders, but which is equally applicable to all believers:

> To be filled with the Spirit means simply that the Christian voluntarily surrenders life and will to the Spirit. Through faith, the believer's personality is filled, mastered and controlled by the Spirit.... To be filled with the Spirit is to be controlled by the Spirit. The Christian leader's mind, emotions, will and physical strength all become available for the Spirit to guide and use.[3]

When the Spirit of God fills you, God takes over the controls of your life. Handing them over is both the hardest and the most liberating thing you can do. But when you do it, giving the Spirit free rein, you discover what it is to know the presence of God and the power of God at work in your life.

[3] J. Oswald Sanders, *Spiritual Leadership* (Chicago: Moody, 1994), pp. 81-82.

CHAPTER SIX

Following Jesus in Everything:
The Essentials of Holiness

Therefore, preparing your minds for action, and being sober-minded, set your hope fully on the grace that will be brought to you at the revelation of Jesus Christ. ¹⁴ As obedient children, do not be conformed to the passions of your former ignorance, ¹⁵ but as he who called you is holy, you also be holy in all your conduct, ¹⁶ since it is written, 'You shall be holy, for I am holy.' ¹⁷ And if you call on him as Father who judges impartially according to each one's deeds, conduct yourselves with fear throughout the time of your exile, ¹⁸ knowing that you were ransomed from the futile ways inherited from your forefathers, not with perishable things such as silver or gold, ¹⁹ but with the precious blood of Christ, like that of a lamb without blemish or spot. ²⁰ He was foreknown before the foundation of the world but was made manifest in the last times for the sake of you ²¹ who through him are believers in God, who raised him from the dead and gave him glory, so that your faith and hope are in God.

²² Having purified your souls by your obedience to the truth for a sincere brotherly love, love one another earnestly from a pure heart, ²³ since you have been born again, not of perishable seed but of imperishable, through the living and abiding word of God; ²⁴ for 'All flesh is like grass and all its glory like the flower of grass. The grass withers, and the flower falls, ²⁵ but the word of the Lord remains for ever.' And this word is the good news that was preached to you. – 1 Peter 1:13-25.

Introduction: good news for the unholy

If you've been a Christian for any length of time, I wonder if you've ever experienced a troubling discrepancy between the way that you know you should live as a Christian, and the way that you actually *do* live. Disciples of Jesus are often conscious, simultaneously, of two things. On the one hand, there are the expectations which the Bible seems to have about the Christian life: expectations of a life of true holiness, real goodness and genuine purity. Over and over again, the Bible teaches unashamedly that this is the life God looks for in his people. But lying side by side with that expectation is your own first-hand experience of the reality of ongoing sin in your life. It can sometimes feel like everyone else in your church has it sorted, whereas you are a very long way from the kind of life that the Bible seems to envisage is normal for a believer.

Does that ring any bells? Maybe you struggle with some particular sin. You've fallen to temptation in the past, you've repented and sought forgiveness, you've been so determined to never repeat it – but somehow, before you know it, you've fallen again. Maybe you've almost reached the point of giving in, as if you've grown helpless to resist sin. It might be a problem with your temper or your tongue: you've tried to control it, but you just keep hurting those you love. Maybe you can't let go of resentment towards another person. You know that the Christian life is characterised by love and grace, and that Christians who have been forgiven should be quick to forgive, and yet the bitterness lingers. Maybe, in common with so many today, you've fallen into sexual sin which can do untold spiritual damage. It could be any of a million things, but what do you do as a believer when you find this discrepancy between how you're supposed to be living and how you're really living?

In this chapter, as we continue to build our picture of Christian discipleship, we're thinking about the basics of holiness. We know that we're called to a life of holiness, but what does that mean? What does it look like? How does it happen?

Let me begin by making something as clear as I possibly can: the gospel is good news for the unholy. Please remember that. The message of the Bible is not, as so many people think, that God loves holy people so you'd better be holy. The message of the Bible is that 'while we were still sinners, Christ died for us' (Romans 5:8). This good news for the unholy has two parts, and the Bible describes them using particular words.

The first part is what we call justification. When we come to Christ in faith, we are 'justified'. That means that we are *counted holy*. The verdict is in, and God declares us forever righteous in his sight. We are right with him. We are not just acceptable, but accepted. This is good news for the unholy, because unholiness leads to death and judgment, but by God's grace we are counted holy and so receive his free gift of eternal life.

The second reason why the gospel is good news for the unholy is what the Bible calls sanctification. Justification means that we've been *declared* holy, but sanctification is the process of being *made* holy. Even as a Christian, sin still 'clings so closely' (Hebrews 12:1). Although God considers us completely holy in Christ, and that can never be taken from us, our lives are still, to a greater or lesser extent, unholy. The great secret is that everyone else is in the same position as you. Not one of us is perfectly holy, and not one of us will ever be perfectly holy this side of glory. We will all sin every day until we die, and so we will all need God's grace every day until we die. Nonetheless, over time we are sanctified, which means that the Holy Spirit works in our lives to transform us so that we come to reflect the likeness of Christ more and more. What is counted true of us *becomes* true of us – gradually, haltingly, imperfectly, but really.

So, if you recognise yourself in the description that I started with, living with that tension between who you should be and who you are, then know this: what the Bible has to say about holiness is not a message of condemnation but of hope. It's the message of a God who has taken hold of you, and will not let you go. The gospel is good news for the unholy (like you and me) because God is in the business of redemption. He loves to take what's broken and make it whole. He specialises in taking what's dirty and making it clean. And when he begins a work in you, he doesn't stop until it's finished.

Spot the difference

You'll maybe remember, probably from childhood, 'spot the difference' puzzles. There are two pictures side by side, very similar at first glance, but if you stop and look a bit more closely, there are numerous tiny differences between them.

So here's the question: what difference does Christ make to our lives? There are two ways we could think about that. The first is to spot the difference between the lives of Christians and non-Christians. That's a complicated thing. We have to bear in mind that all people are created in the image of God, so there is something God-like in all human beings. Even in our fallen condition, we all still reflect something of his goodness, compassion, creativity and so on. That means that any individual Christian won't necessarily be an obviously better person than any individual non-Christian. However, in broad terms there should be a discernible difference between Christians and non-Christians. We are a city on a hill, said Jesus, and unbelievers should see our good works and glorify our Father in heaven (Matthew 5:14-16). In any society, Christians should be living distinctive lives, because the gospel changes us.

But then we know that this happens over time, and being a Christian doesn't make you instantly perfect. C. S. Lewis once pointed out that you have to bear in mind, not only what someone's life and character look like today, but what their starting-point was. If you start off as a thoroughly despicable so-and-so, then maybe being a vaguely decent human being is real progress! So perhaps the better approach is to spot the difference between who you *were* and who you *are*. Has faith in Christ brought about change in your life?

The Bible teaches that saving faith brings about a radical transformation in the life of the believer. We are constantly reminded that, because of Christ, everything is different now. Our perspectives and priorities have changed, our attitudes and lifestyle have changed, our speech and conduct have changed. What we love, what we hate, what we value and what we live for has all changed. As you get to know the New Testament better, you'll see how often it describes the life we used to live, but then reminds us that we no longer walk in those ways. We have a whole new life now.

Have a look at 1 Peter 1:13-25. The Christian's change of life is described at verse 14:

> As obedient children, do not be conformed to the passions of your former ignorance, but as he who called you is holy, you also be holy in all your conduct, since it is written, 'You shall be holy, for I am holy.'

It will certainly take time for faith to permeate our lives, as the implications of the gospel sink deeper and deeper into us. However, if nothing changes – if I continue to think and prioritise and form my views in exactly the same way as my unbelieving neighbour, or if my life looks exactly like it did before I came to know Christ – something is wrong.

We need to understand that holiness is not an optional extra, but part of the gospel itself. If we ask, 'Why did Jesus save us?', the answer is simply, 'Because he loved us.' But if we ask, 'What did Jesus save us *for*?', that's a different question. According to Ephesians 1:4, God chose us before the foundation of the world and saved us 'that we should be holy and blameless before him'. Colossians 1:22 expresses the same reasoning:

> And you, who once were alienated and hostile in mind, doing evil deeds, he has now reconciled in his body of flesh by his death, *in order to present you holy and blameless and above reproach before him*... (emphasis added).

From eternity past, it has been God's purpose to create for himself a holy people. This is why it's so important that we should seek holiness, and why we can do so with real hope.

So the prospect of real change is held out to us. You may have heard the wonderful statement reported to have been uttered by John Newton, whose life changed beyond all recognition, from the eighteenth century slave trader to minister of the gospel:

> … though I am not what I ought to be, nor what I wish to be, nor what I hope to be, I can truly say, I am not what I once was; a slave to sin and Satan; and I can heartily join with the apostle, and acknowledge, 'By the grace of God I am what I am.'

Through the gospel, there is the prospect of real change, so that more and more we can spot the difference that Christ makes.

What does change look like?

So what does this change look like? We've been happily talking about holiness, but what is it? Strangely, it doesn't have a good press. In one of its more spectacular instances of turning moral truth on its head, modern Western culture has turned holiness into something to be despised and avoided. At worst, it's reprehensible: it's associated with being holier-than-thou, and has connotations of self-righteousness and judgmentalism and hypocrisy. At best, it's well-meaning but ultimately dull. Holiness is boring. It's for staid people who don't know how to have fun. The Puritans were fine Christians with a concern for holiness of life, but today's culture would agree with the atheist H. L. Mencken's jibe that Puritanism can be defined as the haunting fear that someone, somewhere may be enjoying themselves. Now that might be funny, but is it true? Is holiness really all about not doing what you want to do, and having to do what you don't? Is it really about keeping the reins on happiness?

Here's an interesting fact: Christians of a previous age believed exactly the opposite. Not only is holiness compatible with happiness, but holiness is the key to happiness. This is what Scottish pastor Robert Murray M'Cheyne wrote to a fellow-minister: 'Never cease to show your people that to be holy is to be happy; and that to bring us to perfect holiness and likeness to God, was the very end for which Christ died.'[1] On a different occasion he wrote:

> To gain entire likeness to Christ, I ought to get a high esteem of the happiness of it. I am persuaded that God's happiness is insepa-rably linked in with his holiness. Holiness and happiness are like light and heat. God never tasted one of the pleasures of sin. Christ had a body such as I have, yet He never tasted one of the pleasures of sin. The redeemed, through all eternity, will never taste one of the pleasures of sin; yet their happiness is complete. It would be my greatest happiness to be from this moment entirely like them. Every sin is something away from my greatest enjoyment… . The devil strives night and day to make me forget this or disbelieve it.[2]

The devil has been hard at work in our generation. People today would laugh at the notion that the key to happiness is to be found in holiness. I suspect many Christians would have trouble comprehending it. How can this be true?

We need to begin by reclaiming the word itself, so that we can under-stand what holiness truly is. When you drill down to the foundations of it, holiness is not about 'doing good things' or 'not doing bad things'. It's something far deeper, greater and more glorious. We begin by recognis-ing that God himself is 'holy' in a supreme sense. This means that he is 'above and beyond anything in the universe'.[3] He is separate from his creation, and completely untainted by its fallenness. Peter Lewis says:

> … when God himself approaches any of his creatures to reveal himself to them, the first and chief thing he wants them to know about himself is that he is holy… It is difficult to give the term 'holy' any one meaning, as it is a description of what God is in

---

[1] *Memoir and Remains of R. M. M'Cheyne*, Andrew Bonar (London: Banner of Truth Trust, 1966), p. 269.
[2] *Ibid.*, p. 154.
[3] R. C. Sproul, *Everyone's a Theologian*, p. 66.

himself in his infinite perfection. It is not one thing about God, but everything about God. It is the most fundamental feature of the divine being and it is the total glory of all he is; it underlies and characterises every attribute and it is the sum of all his attributes. Out of his holy being all his deeds and decisions proceed: his speech is the announcement of his holiness, his glory is the display of his holiness, his wrath is the revulsion of his holiness against sin, and his love is the embrace by his holiness of all that is good and true.[4]

Next, think about how the word 'holiness' has come to be used in history. Your Bible probably says on the front or down the spine, 'Holy Bible'. The land of Israel is often referred to as 'the Holy Land', and Jerusalem is 'the Holy City'. What do these things have in common? It's simple: they belong to God. Everything does, of course, but in a special sense, these are his: his book, his land, his city.

Now, says Peter, 'you also be holy' (1 Peter 1:15). In other words, be his. It's not about having a big list of do's and don'ts. It's not about beating others in a goody-two-shoes competition. It's about cultivating an attitude of heart and mind and spirit that says to God, 'I belong to you. I am yours – at every moment, in every way, with all I am and all I have.' Do you see how holiness goes far beyond 'being good' and into the deepest questions of our lives: who we are, what we live for, our purpose and our passion? Peter doesn't say, 'do holy things'; he says, 'be holy in all your conduct'. Overarching the whole of our lives is the total commitment of doing everything for the purpose of God. When we pursue holiness, we're saying to God: 'I set my hope on you. I want what you want. Most of all, I want you, and I cast aside everything that would distract me from you. By your grace and your strength, I will dedicate my life to your purpose.'

Therefore we take Christ with us into every part of our lives, and there reflect his character. The pattern is: 'You shall be holy, for I

[4] Peter Lewis, *The Glory of Christ* (Carlisle: Paternoster, 2001), pp. 259-260.

am holy.' Sanctification is the process of becoming more like him, and it's in the ordinary day-to-day things of life where we discover to what extent our hearts have really changed. Kevin DeYoung has a striking expression: he describes holiness as 'the sum of a million little things'. It's not about a single moment of decision, but all the decisions that make up our lives.

> Holiness is the sum of a million little things – the avoidance of little evils and little foibles, the setting aside of little bits of worldliness and little acts of compromise, the putting to death of little inconsistencies and little indiscretions, the attention to little duties and little dealings, the hard work of little self-denials and little self-restraints, the cultivation of little benevolences and little forbearances. Are you trustworthy? Are you kind? Are you patient? Are you joyful? Do you love? These qualities, worked out in all the little things of life, determine whether you are blight or blessing to everyone around you.…[5]

Holiness is immensely practical, but it only becomes practical when it truly has sunk deep into us as a fundamental reorientation of our hearts. God is so gracious in this. He looks for our obedience, but he doesn't frighten or coerce us into it. Instead he makes it the desire of our hearts. The paradox is that it's as we surrender everything to him, dedicating ourselves to holiness, that we find true happiness – because it's then that we are living the life that we were created to live.

Hang on a minute: what about God's law?

Good question – I'm glad you've asked it! If holiness is a matter of God changing our hearts rather than mere obedience to external commands, does that mean we can jettison a good proportion of the Bible? All those Old Testament laws surely don't have anything to do with Christians today, do they? In fact, doesn't Paul say in Romans 6:14 that we are 'not under the law'? Yes, he does – but that

[5] Kevin DeYoung, *The Hole in our Holiness* (Wheaton: Crossway, 2012), p. 145.

happens to be one of the most misunderstood verses in the Bible, and the law of God happens to be one of the most misunderstood subjects in theology.

To explore the Christian's relationship to the law of God would take another book, but for our present purposes we need to know that God's law is divided into three parts.

1. The Old Testament contains the *civil laws of Israel*. Since God's people existed as a nation state, they needed a legal code to govern their life, settle disputes, punish criminals and so on. These laws of ancient Israel are not binding on us for the same reason that the laws of Bolivia aren't binding on us: we're not Bolivians. If you happen to be Bolivian… well, you get the point. We're not bound by the laws of ancient Israel because we're not ancient Israelites. However, while these parts of God's law might not be directly binding on Christians as such, that doesn't mean that we can't learn from them about the character of God and his concern for the wellbeing of his people. You just don't have to consult the Bible to know what to do if your neighbour's ox falls into a pit on your land (Exodus 21:33-34).

2. The Old Testament also contains the *ceremonial laws of the sacrificial system*. These have all been fulfilled in Christ, who offered himself as the final, perfect sacrifice from God for God, and these laws are therefore not binding on Christians. However, that doesn't mean that we can't learn from them about the character of God and how he taught his people the meaning of holiness. You just don't have to worry if your favourite restaurant serves up a fine camel steak or fillet of rock badger (Deuteronomy 14:7).

3. Finally, the Old Testament contains the *moral law of God*. These are laws in which God tells us what is right and wrong, and commands our obedience. Since these laws reflect the very character of God, and the unchanging nature of the moral reality which he has established, they remain binding on the Christian. There are many examples, but the most basic are the Ten Commandments, recorded in Exodus 20:3-17. These are so foundational that I'd recommend

you take the time to both meditate on them and to memorise them. Please notice, however, that even here in the Old Testament, the Ten Commandments come *after* the statement, 'I am the LORD your God, who brought you out of the land of Egypt, out of the house of slavery.' The order is everything. God's law comes to us, not so that we can be saved by keeping it, but so that we can respond in glad obedience to the God who has already redeemed us from our slavery to sin. Contrary to what most unbelievers assume the Christian faith teaches, obedience is not the cause of salvation but the result of it.

What then did Paul mean when he said in Romans 6:14 that we are 'not under law but under grace'? I think he's saying that, before we come to Christ, we are 'under' the law in the sense that it demands perfect obedience of us, and condemns us when we fail. We are 'under' it in the terrible sense of being under its condemnation, but it can do nothing to save us. But when we come to Christ, the condemnation of the law is lifted from us: we are no longer *condemned under the law*, but are *saved under grace*. This certainly does not mean that we can now ignore what God says about what is right and wrong, and in fact the context of the verse is that the gospel has set us free from the power of sin in order that we can live righteous lives. Paul gives thanks to God, therefore, that the Christians in Rome have become 'obedient from the heart' to the teaching they have received (Romans 6:17).

Today, the moral law has three functions:

1. It shows us who we were designed to be as people, and so restrains evil in the world by means of conscience.

2. It shows us who we are, as sinners, and so drives us to Christ for forgiveness.

3. It shows us who we are to become, as Christ's people, and so nurtures our holiness.

For all these reasons, the law of God, properly understood, is immensely precious to the Christian. Far from setting up law and love as opposites, as so many do today, we should understand how the law of God helps us to love him and others, and trains us in holiness. The commandments of God help us to offer rich, deep, glad, free, joyful, Christ-reflecting, God-glorifying obedience by the power of Jesus at work in us. I hope that, as you come to know God's law more and more, you will discover the truth of the paradox that is described by J. I. Packer: the Christian who dips his toe into it finds the water cold and uninviting, but the one who jumps in discovers that the water's lovely![6]

How does change come?

We've seen that holiness is a change in the desires of our hearts, leading to a change in the conduct of our lives. How does this come about? Let me tell you first how it doesn't come. It doesn't come because Christians are better people than others, or because they try harder than others, or because they've turned over a new leaf, or because they've discovered a special means of moral improvement or spiritual development. Peter tells us how it comes.

> Blessed be the God and Father of our Lord Jesus Christ! According-
> ing to his great mercy, he has caused us to be born again to a living
> hope... (1 Peter 1:3).

Do you get the point of that image? Becoming a Christian isn't about taking my life and upgrading it to a better version: (in my case) Randall 2.0. It's not like adding some extra memory to my laptop to make it run faster. It's about the most radical break with the past. It's about the end of one life and the beginning of another. What could be more radical than new birth? He has caused us to be born again so that, as Paul puts it so gloriously in 2 Corinthians 5:17, 'if anyone is in Christ, he is a new creation. The old has passed away; behold, the new has come.' Remember what we saw in the last chapter: the reason any of us becomes a Christian is not that

---

[6] J. I. Packer, *Keeping the Ten Commandments* (Wheaton: Crossway, 2007), p. 112.

we brilliantly perceive the truth all of a sudden, but that the Holy Spirit performs a kind of heart surgery on us. He removes our old, hard, unbelieving heart and transplants a new, soft, receptive heart into us. The gospel, which looked like foolishness before, is now revealed as the supreme wisdom of God. The cross of Christ, which had always looked like weakness, is revealed as power.

From there everything changes, because there's a new heart beating in us. You may have believed in the past that the Christian faith is all about God making demands of us: you must do this, you mustn't do that, because that is what God wants. Tragically, many people live as if that were the heart of faith. Many people in our churches have been led to believe that it is. Maybe you become a Christian by God's grace, but then it's over to you, isn't it? Now you just have to try really hard to live the way God wants you to live, don't you?

Don't misunderstand me. God is God, and he makes demands of us, and he has every right to. What's more, those demands are limitless. He asks that we hand over our lives to him. But the thing that transforms our experience of the Christian life is when we come to grasp its true dynamic. When we misunderstand holiness, and see it as fundamentally something that we have to achieve, we spend our lives saying: 'I have to live a new life.' When we fail, we scold ourselves – sometimes we loathe ourselves – and we look in the mirror, and with dread in our hearts we repeat, 'I have to live a new life.' Every time we fall, the sense of hopelessness and failure rises as for endless years we repeat this increasingly desperate mantra: 'I have to live a new life.'

The true dynamic of the Christian life is: 'I have a new life to live.' That's a different thing altogether. I have been given a new life. It's not mine, it's the life of God placed within me. It's his heartbeat in my soul.

Every other religion in the world is a variation on the theme of self-improvement. The essence of the message is this: 'Be what you're not. Become better than you are. Improve yourself. Pull yourself up by your own ethical bootstraps. Try harder. You can do it.' It's the moral equivalent, if you know the story, of *The Little Engine That Could*. The other engines say it's too hard to pull all the carriages up the hill but the little engine has a go. As he strains and strains and slowly climbs, he says to himself, over and over, 'I think I can, I think I can, I think I can….' That's what religion is like. That's what non-Christian ethics is like. Can I do better? Can I improve? Can I climb this moral mountain? I think I can, I think I can… I hope I can. I'm sure if I try hard enough, I can be what I'm not. But of course, none of us can. We can be only be who we are.

The power of the gospel is that *it changes who we are*. There's a new heart beating in us. We've been born again into a new life. We have a new identity in Christ. That means that the message of the Bible about holiness, and the reason holiness is good news, is this: the Bible tells us, over and over again, to be what we are.[7] Is that not a great relief? God doesn't ask you to be what you're not. Instead, he changes you by placing his life within you and then he asks you to be what, by his grace, you now are. This is amazing grace: what he asks of you, he gives to you. As Iain Murray puts it, 'For the person who fears and loves God, the command "Be ye holy, for I am holy", is not grievous. Rather it corresponds with an inmost desire.'[8]

This doesn't mean that obedience is suddenly easy and the battle with sin is over, but it does tell us something important about how to fight it. If you struggle with a particular behaviour, your great need is not to focus on overcoming it, but to focus on your relationship with Jesus Christ and the new identity that you have in him. Everything else flows from that. Draw close to him. Become what you are in him. Over time, by God's grace, your new identity will become more and more real to you, and the life of the gospel will

---

[7] I have to credit a sermon of Alistair Begg of Parkside Church, Ohio as the source of the contrast between the demand to be who we're not and the demand to be who we are.

[8] Iain H. Murray, *Seven Leaders* (Edinburgh: Banner of Truth Trust, 2017), p. 23.

become more and more instinctive. To begin with, though, you'll have to be conscious and deliberate in reminding yourself of who you are now in Christ. When you sense the pull of temptation, what do you need to do? You need to remind yourself, consciously, of who you are. Say it out loud if it helps. Say to yourself: 'This reaction, this attitude, this behaviour is not who I am. At one time this would have made sense as the natural outflow of my sin-enslaved heart, but not now. I'm a new person. I've been born again into a new life. I'm a new creation. I belong to Jesus Christ. At the price of his precious blood, I have been redeemed from emptiness and futility and slavery to sin. I am free. I do not have to sin any longer. I am one of God's children, chosen by him for obedience to Jesus Christ. This is who I am, and now in this moment of decision I choose to be who I am.'

Conclusion: live your new life

We need to remind ourselves of these truths all the time, and then we need to maintain a very difficult balance. On the one hand we should look for and expect real holiness. We should make no excuses for sin. On the other hand, we should recognise that there will still be times when we fail, and we should always remember that the gospel is good news for the unholy.

The key thing in pursuing true holiness of life is to remember the new life that is now yours in Christ. In a verse that is well worth committing to memory, Paul writes:

> I have been crucified with Christ. It is no longer I who live, but Christ who lives in me. And the life I now live in the flesh, I live by faith in the Son of God who loved me and gave himself for me (Galatians 2:20).

What's the difference? *He* is.

CHAPTER SEVEN

Following Jesus More and More:
The Essentials of Growth

And he gave the apostles, the prophets, the evangelists, the shepherds and teachers, [12] to equip the saints for the work of ministry, for building up the body of Christ, [13] until we all attain to the unity of the faith and of the knowledge of the Son of God, to mature manhood, to the measure of the stature of the fullness of Christ, [14] so that we may no longer be children, tossed to and fro by the waves and carried about by every wind of doctrine, by human cunning, by craftiness in deceitful schemes. [15] Rather, speaking the truth in love, we are to grow up in every way into him who is the head, into Christ, [16] from whom the whole body, joined and held together by every joint with which it is equipped, when each part is working properly, makes the body grow so that it builds itself up in love.

[17] Now this I say and testify in the Lord, that you must no longer walk as the Gentiles do, in the futility of their minds. [18] They are darkened in their understanding, alienated from the life of God because of the ignorance that is in them, due to their hardness of heart. [19] They have become callous and have given themselves up to sensuality, greedy to practise every kind of impurity. [20] But that is not the way you learned Christ! – [21] assuming that you have heard about him and were taught in him, as the truth is in Jesus, [22] to put off your old self, which belongs to your former manner of life and is corrupt through deceitful desires, [23] and to be renewed in the spirit of your minds, [24] and to put on the new self, created after the likeness of God in true righteousness and holiness. – Ephesians 4:11-24.

Introduction: grow up!

His name was Pepe. Well it wasn't really, but for reasons that are lost in the mists of time, that's what we called him. It was primary school, and there was a boy in my class who was tiny. I can still picture him from class photos. We were all pretty small at the time, of course, but Pepe just didn't seem to grow with the rest of us. Within a few years the doctors were worried enough that he was receiving growth hormone injections. His lack of growth was a concern that needed intervention.

Growth is a sign of health, and a lack of growth in just about any living thing is an indication that something is wrong. As human beings, our physical growth will eventually stop – we might even shrink a bit – but even then, in more significant ways we continue to grow as people until we die.

The Bible is always deeply concerned about the growth of Christian believers, and all Christians should make it their ambition to make progress in faith continually until the day they die. More than that, they should intentionally plan to make that happen. When Paul wrote to the churches in the early years of the Christian faith, he made it clear that it mattered enormously to him that they should become more and more mature in their faith. Writing to the Christians in Colossae (in what is now Turkey), he sets out his great ambition for all the churches that he serves:

> [Christ] we proclaim, warning everyone and teaching everyone with all wisdom, that we may present everyone mature in Christ. For this I toil, struggling with all his energy that he powerfully works within me (Colossians 1:28-29).

Paul wants the body of Christ to be built up 'until we all attain to the unity of the faith and of the knowledge of the Son of God, to mature manhood, to the measure of the stature of the fullness of Christ' (Ephesians 4:13). He wants Christians to 'grow up in every way into him who is the head, into Christ' (verse 15), and longs that the church might grow as it 'builds itself up in love' (verse 16).

The biblical vision of the normal Christian life is not that we come to faith and then we put our spiritual feet up and wait for heaven. We should long for growth, and actively pursue maturity in faith and discipleship.

Although this book is about the *basics* of Christian discipleship, growth is one of the basics! In the end, it's about following Jesus more and more – and there is not one of us, no matter how long or short a time we've been a believer, who follows Jesus as we should. There is not one of us who can be satisfied with our spiritual condition or commitment. If we are, that is simply further proof of our immaturity. The paradox is that, as people grow in faith, one of the things they become more aware of is how much more they still need to grow in faith.

Just think for a moment about what spiritual immaturity would look like. If spiritual immaturity was prevalent in the church, what would we expect to see? We'd expect to see believers who don't really know their Bibles; a church uncertain of what it believes; church leaders failing in their responsibility to lead faithfully and set an example for the flock; a church meekly falling into line with whatever the unbelieving culture thinks, rather than being shaped by what God's word says; believers who aren't really committed to personal or corporate prayer; believers not really equipped to contend for the faith, or to give an answer for the hope that is in them; a widespread falling-away of young people who were brought up in the church; and, above all, decline. We'd expect to see ageing congregations, with churches shrinking and closing.

Sadly, much of the modern Western church falls squarely within that description. But God has given us all the resources we need to set a different course and to grow in understanding, maturity, wisdom, confidence and godliness. In this chapter, focussing on Ephesians 4:11-24, we'll see how Paul paints a picture of growing Christians and a growing church. The gospel has not changed, and the power of God has not lessened, since he wrote these words.

So in the interests of avoiding the kind of stunted growth that was such a problem for my friend at school, let's consider four key things which take us away from decline and death, and point us instead to life and growth. Here are our spiritual 'growth-hormone' injections: Paul envisages the word at work, equipping for ministry, building the community, resulting in stability.

The word at work (verse 11)

The first principle, which can never be stressed too strongly, is that growth in the Christian life comes from the word at work. To ensure the birth and growth of his people, God gave 'the apostles, the prophets, the evangelists, the pastors and teachers...' (verse 11). Paul mentions these people specifically, not because they are more important than other Christians, but because their role is to teach the Christian faith and therefore to encourage growth in all believers.

Paul mentions the apostles and prophets. The apostles were the individuals who were directly and personally commissioned by the risen Christ to be his first witnesses to the world – namely the twelve disciples, minus Judas who betrayed Jesus and killed himself, plus Paul who was commissioned by Christ on the road to Damascus (Acts 9). The prophets were those whom God appointed to speak to his people before his written word had been completed. Because we now have the whole Bible, which is God's sufficient word, God no longer appoints apostles and prophets in the church today. In fact, in Ephesians 2:20, Paul describes the church as being 'built on the foundation of the apostles and prophets'. In other words, through them God laid the foundation of our faith. Through them he communicated the gospel to us, and he caused his word to be written down, and in due time completed and then closed. The remaining gifts mentioned in verse 11 are given to put that completed word to work in the church. Some are gifted as evangelists, with a particular role to make the gospel known to unbelievers. Others are gifted as pastor-teachers (the grammar suggests that the same people are performing both of those roles) who take the word of God and apply it to the lives of the people. They do not add anything new. You should not expect to hear new revelation from God as you go to church week by week, but rather the explanation and application of what God has revealed once-for-all in the Scriptures.

It is the word of God that brings growth towards Christian maturity.

The significance of this is very obvious. If you want to grow as a Christian, you need to put the word of God to work in your life. That means being regular in your church attendance, and rejecting other things that would keep you from meeting with your fellow-believers. It means encouraging one another and learning together from God's word. It means taking the opportunities for growth that are given, some of which I have already mentioned. If your church has an evening service, that's another great opportunity to grow in faith, lingering at the feet of Christ, learning from him. Make it a habit to read a part of the Bible every day. Use Bible-reading notes or books that are helpful, but take hold of a part of the Scriptural text and take it with you into your day. Memorise as much of the Bible as you can. You might be the kind of person who can memorise the book of Isaiah in an afternoon, or you might struggle to remember single verses, but it's worth memorising as much or as little as you can. It's valuable to memorise the books of the Bible in order, so that you can find your way around your Bible more easily. Read good books that are committed to the authority of the Bible and that teach it well. With careful discernment, and with some help from more mature Christians whose judgment you trust, find online resources that can help you to think more deeply about your faith. Think through, deliberately, how your faith applies to every aspect of your life: your work, your family life, your leisure time, your parenting, your finances – everything. I hope this book will help you to do that.

As you do this, remember always that the point of it all is not to cram facts into your head, but for you to know God better. Christian growth is about growing in a relationship. You're getting to know God more and more, through Christ. You meet with him in his word. You meet with him on your knees too, which is why this book has a chapter on prayer, another key to spiritual growth.

As Paul speaks in Ephesians 4 about how believers are to grow, his starting point is the word of God applied to us, sinking into us, shaping us.

Equipping for ministry (verse 12)

We then discover that, although there is a kind of 'ministry' which is to be undertaken by the man we call the 'minister', his role is to equip the whole church to perform ministry in a broader sense. According to verse 12, the evangelists and pastor-teachers are given 'to equip the saints for the work of ministry, for building up the body of Christ'.

So for all of us, growth comes not just through learning, but through doing. Christians grow as they serve, doing the work that God has given them. The pastor-teacher 'equips', which is a word that implies not just teaching, but training. This is the kind of teaching that enables someone to fulfil a role, giving them the spiritual 'equipment' they'll need. This is another reminder that as we come to God's word week by week, we're not just cramming facts into our heads, but training to live in a certain way.

This whole section of Ephesians emphasises the need for Christians to exercise the gifts that God has given them. In fact Paul says something amazing in verse 7, about grace being given to each one of us 'according to the measure of Christ's gift'. That means that Jesus Christ himself has looked upon your church and has assessed its needs; and he has then looked upon every single one of its members, and has measured out to them all the gifts they need to serve him there. Some are great at getting alongside others, listening, and helping others to work through issues. Some are terrified by that kind of thing, but can work skilfully with their hands and create amazing things to the glory of God. Some relate to teenagers very well, while for others the world of the teenager is an alien land they have never visited and a foreign language they have never learned. God gives to his church academic gifts, gifts of encouragement, generosity, service, prayer, speaking – a million different things, measured out to us according to our need. We grow in faith as we use these gifts. Christ himself has placed them in our hands, and we grow as we use them for the blessing of others and for the glory of his name.

In the Bible, the church is a bit like an orchestra. There are hundreds of different instruments. They come in and out of the melody at different times, and some are more prominent or louder than others, but they all have their part to play. By our selfish human nature, none of us wants to play second fiddle. We all want the brilliant solo performance, but as long as we think in terms of 'my right to use my gift', the orchestra will produce what we call *cacophony* (which is a Greek word meaning 'bad sound'). Only as we truly seek to serve one another, and look together to the Conductor, will he take this cacophony and transform into a glorious *symphony* (which is a Greek word meaning 'together sound').

In that process we grow. It really doesn't matter whether you have a wonderful violin solo, or whether you're the percussionist who has to sit with the triangle and wait for twenty minutes and then, at just the right moment – *ting!* What matters is that we make music together to the glory of God.

Building the community (verse 13)

Paul's vision continues to build in verse 13: he sees the word at work, equipping God's people for ministry, and therefore building the community. As individuals grow, the 'body of Christ' grows, 'until we all attain to the unity of the faith and of the knowledge of the

Son of God, to mature manhood, to the measure of the stature of the fullness of Christ'. We've already seen this passage pick up on many of the themes that we've touched on in this book (faith, the Bible, holiness, prayer), and here it picks up on another: the church. We grow together. Paul makes a very clear and direct connection between Christian maturity and Christian unity.

Notice how Paul describes this unity. It is 'the unity of the faith and of the knowledge of the Son of God'. We are united as we commit together to the content of the Christian confession as defined by God's word, and as we love the Christ we find there. This is the only possible basis of Christian unity. Where the Bible is rejected, or where a church tries to redefine who Christ is, unity is not possible and growth is stunted. The word of God gives content to the gospel, the gospel unites us, and in that unity we grow. Therefore if we want to grow as Christians, we need to commit to the truth of the Bible ourselves and we need to find a church community in which others do the same. Paul makes clear that Christian maturity cannot be separated from Christian unity. In his mind, it all goes together: we attain to unity, to mature manhood, and to the measure of the stature of the fullness of Christ.

It makes perfect sense that growth happens in community. Growth is about getting to know Christ better, and together we will always see and understand more of Christ than any of us would do alone. This is one of the most valuable things about Bible study groups, and about being able to speak openly with other Christians about your faith. You go to a Bible study, and someone says something, and you think, 'Why did I never see that before?' Your view of Jesus is enriched. You say something, which might seem obvious to you, but someone else is thinking, 'I never thought of that.' In this way we grow together more than we could ever grow alone.

The word of God is at work in a Bible-believing church, equipping for ministry and building the community together. Standing side by side in the gospel, we stretch one another, we encourage one another, and we build one another up.

Resulting in stability (verse 14)

As a result of the word, and each others' ministry, we become more stable in our faith. Paul says at verse 14 that we grow to maturity 'so that we may no longer be children, tossed to and fro by the waves and carried about by every wind of doctrine, by human cunning, by craftiness in deceitful schemes'.

I grew up in a fishing village in the north-east of Scotland, and there were times when it was genuinely terrifying to watch the boats head out into the North Sea. You could get sea-sick just looking at them as they lurched in every direction, and were tossed around by the waves. That's what an immature believer or church is like, according to Paul, defenceless against the storms of false thinking and false belief which are so deadly to the spiritual life. From the beginning, the Christian faith has always had to contend against those who would seek to undermine it, sometimes from the outside but often from the inside. 'Oh, you don't have to believe that Jesus was really God… the Resurrection was just a spiritual thing, not a physical thing… we don't need to believe any more what the Bible says about…' and so on. We need maturity in order to be able to stand firm when we are battered by the winds of false doctrine, by human cunning that would undermine God's word, and by the craftiness of deceitful schemes.

Conclusion: growing up into Christ

Let me leave you with one last thing that Paul says about Christian growth. It may seem obvious to say that Christian growth is a thoroughly Christ-centred thing, but notice the way he puts it at verse 15: 'Rather, speaking the truth in love, we are to grow up in every way into him who is the head, into Christ….' This is not mainly growth into greater knowledge, although that is part of it. It's not mainly growth into greater obedience, although that comes with it. It's growth into *Christ himself*. It's growth into closer relationship with him, and deeper understanding of who he is and how he thinks and what he desires and what will honour him. It's growth into greater Christ-likeness.

There's a wonderful moment in *Prince Caspian* (one of C. S. Lewis's *Chronicles of Narnia*) when Lucy encounters Aslan, the Christ-figure, having not seen him for a while:

> 'Aslan,' said Lucy, 'you're bigger.'
> 'That is because you are older, little one', answered he.
> 'Not because you are?'
> 'I am not. But every year you grow, you will find me bigger.'[1]

That is what it means to grow as a Christian. As we grow, Christ gets bigger – or rather, our vision of Christ expands, and our capacity to see him enlarges, so that we come to see more and more of the reality of who he is, and who he has been all along. We find in him greater glory, deeper love, more satisfying joy than we ever thought possible. There is so much more of him to know, and growing in that knowledge is its own reward.

[1] C. S. Lewis, *Prince Caspian* (London: Harper Collins, 1980), p. 124.

CHAPTER EIGHT

Following Jesus in Our Choices:
The Essentials of Guidance

Rejoice always, [17] pray without ceasing, [18] give thanks in all circumstances; for this is the will of God in Christ Jesus for you. [19] Do not quench the Spirit. [20] Do not despise prophecies, [21] but test everything; hold fast what is good. [22] Abstain from every form of evil. – 1 Thessalonians 5:16-22.

I appeal to you therefore, brothers, by the mercies of God, to present your bodies as a living sacrifice, holy and acceptable to God, which is your spiritual worship. [2] Do not be conformed to this world, but be transformed by the renewal of your mind, that by testing you may discern what is the will of God, what is good and acceptable and perfect. – Romans 12:1-2.

Introduction: how do I know?

God's will for our lives is a great mystery. He knows exactly what he wants for us, including all of our decisions, and especially the big ones, but he's hiding it from us to see if we can figure it out. If we figure it out, we'll be 'right in the centre of his will'. If we don't, we'll miss out on 'God's best for us'. Does that sound right to you?

You may be relieved to hear that it's not. That is far from a biblical view of God (who is not cruel or capricious), and of the way God guides us (which is not like a cryptic puzzle). The little nugget of truth that can make it sound plausible is that God does have a sovereign will which overrules every detail of life, through which he governs everything that happens from eternity past to eternity future. However, he does not intend for us to know his sovereign will for the simple reason that we can't. We don't have the capacity to understand the world as God does. What God intends for us is not that we should try to discover his *hidden* will, but that we should live by his *revealed* will. This makes all the difference in the world. It relieves Christians of the burden of trying to discern things they were never intended to know. It takes from us the guilty suspicion that all other Christians are more spiritual than we are, since they seem to be able to hear messages from God that we don't hear. It also makes it possible and practical to 'discern what is the will of God' (Romans 12:2).

It's true, of course, that in the Bible we see God making his purposes known in some pretty extraordinary ways. There are prophets who receive messages directly from God. There are words of knowledge (although we're not certain what they were) and gifts of tongues (although we're not certain what they were either). God speaks to people in dreams and visions, and sometimes even in an audible voice. So is that how we should expect God to guide us today? Can we just assume that he will do for us today what he did for others in the past? I want to encourage you to challenge that assumption, particularly because something profoundly important has happened between then and now. That event was the completion of the Bible. By definition, everything we read of in the Bible occurred before the Bible had been completed. God was in the process of planning and then performing his amazing work of salvation, and then establishing his church in the world for the first time. It's not hard to see why he might use unusual methods to do that foundational work. As we saw in Chapter 7, he even tells us in Ephesians 2:20 that the church is 'built on the foundation of the apostles and prophets'. I'm no civil engineer, but I'm pretty sure that foundations are designed to be built once and then left alone. In fact, tampering with the foundation is a sure way to undermine a building.

The testimony of the apostles and prophets has been written down for us in the Bible. As we saw in Chapter 2, the Bible itself tells us that it speaks with the voice of God in a way that nothing else does. It bears a unique authority, and is sufficient for our lives as Christians. That means that the completion of the Bible marked a momentous event in history. God had now delivered his word to humanity, a word which was to be complete and sufficient for all time.

This means that we should not now expect God to guide us by means of direct supernatural messages which tell us what to do, and what not to do. I have known Christians who have been almost paralysed because they had no confidence to do anything until they had some ill-defined experience of 'hearing God's will' for them. They would wait for signs from heaven, or internal 'impressions' which they judged to be from the Holy Spirit. They usually ended up making decisions on the basis that 'I just feel a real peace about it' – which is a deeply dangerous thing for a sin-infested creature to do. People have claimed to feel 'a real peace' about all manner of wickedness! To say that such an approach is not biblical does not imply for a moment that God is any less powerful today, or any less active, than he was in the past. In fact we'll discover shortly that, rather than directly telling us what to do, God has a far *more* wonderful way of guiding his people today.

So how *does* God guide us today? How should you expect to see him working in your life, ordinarily and regularly, to guide your decisions and actions?

Things you don't need to ask God about

Strange as it may seem, our starting point in considering the basics of guidance is to recognise that there are many areas where we don't *need* to seek the guidance of God. I don't mean that you don't need his guidance, but simply that you don't need to go hunting around for it because he's already told you. God gave us the Bible for one main reason: to show us Jesus, and his work of salvation in the gospel. But he also gave it to us to tell us how he wants us to live, and there's a huge amount of guidance already there for us in black and white which we must be careful to heed.

Let me put it this way. If you ever find yourself praying about whether God wants you to have an affair with your colleague at work, something has gone wrong in your Christian life. Neither do you need to pray about whether it's alright to disrespect your parents, gossip, use the Lord's name carelessly, conjure up the spirits of the dead, or get drunk on the office night out. If you're looking for guidance in these areas, you just need to clear some space in your diary and get to know your Bible better.

Those may be blindingly obvious examples, but the specific commands of the Bible are a hugely important starting-point as we consider the guidance of God. God *has guided* us. If we ignore the guidance he has provided, it is not reasonable to expect him to guide us further.

Revealed: the will of God for your life

I hope the examples I gave above were obvious to you, but it's amazing the capacity we have to ignore many other things that the Bible has already revealed about God's will for our lives. We're going to take 1 Thessalonians 5:16-22 as an example, but there are many other passages of a similar nature and you'll be able to apply their teaching yourself in the same way. The Christians in Thessalonica, however, were in the same position as many readers of this book: they were new Christians, who were recently converted and looking to grow in their faith.

I once had a friend who seemed to spend his entire life studying. As he moved from one degree to the next, I remember him saying over and over again, 'I'm just trying to work out what God wants for my life.' This went on for years, certainly into his fifties, and it got harder and harder to resist responding, 'Look, I think you'd better hurry up!' He had fallen victim to the assumptions I mentioned at the start of this chapter, that God knows every specific decision he wants us to make but for some reason has hidden his will from us. If you've been tempted to think in that way, let me tell you something amazing: in 1 Thessalonians 5:18, Paul tells us in so many words what is 'the will of God in Christ Jesus for you'. It's like a breaking news report: 'We can exclusively reveal the will of God for your life!' If this is true, it's great news. We can stop searching and start reading. My friend can be helped to move on.

So what are Paul's next words? Let me tell you first what he doesn't say. He doesn't say that the will of God for you is that you should be a librarian, marry Deirdre (or Bob) from church, buy a house in the suburbs and have six children. That is just not Paul's way of thinking, and I don't believe it's God's way of thinking. His guidance is usually more like a compass than a road map. He doesn't have a specific route marked out for us, with every twist and turn set in advance in his mind as a moral imperative. Instead, there's a direction in which we need to travel. That's immensely liberating, because it frees us to make good and godly decisions without the nagging sense that we might be 'getting it wrong'.

The standing orders of the gospel

So what does Paul tell us is 'the will of God in Christ Jesus for you'?

> Rejoice always, pray without ceasing, give thanks in all circum-
> stances… (1 Thessalonians 5:16-18).

Someone has described these three commands in the above verses as 'the standing orders of the gospel'.[1] In the army, a 'standing order' is a general order which remains in force. It always applies,

[1] James Denney, quoted in Geoffrey B. Wilson, *New Testament Commentaries*, vol. 2 (Edinburgh: Banner of Truth Trust, 2005), p. 177.

all the time, in every circumstance. Whenever any behaviour is governed by standing orders, you don't need to wonder what to do. You don't need to work it out. You just need to do whatever your standing orders tell you. Here Paul sets out some of the standing orders which are implicit in the gospel. They apply to all Christians at all times and in all circumstances. They're standing orders of the *gospel* because they depend on the gospel, flow out of the gospel, only make sense in the light of the gospel, and can only be obeyed through the work of the gospel.

So these are attitudes of heart that should characterise all Christians at all times. This is what God wants us to do, *whatever* we're doing. First, we are to have an attitude of joy, not in a shallow sense but in the sense of the deep joy in Christ which is the birth-right of every Christian. This is possible because we're not those who rejoice in our circumstances, but who rejoice 'in the Lord' (Philippians 4:4). Gospel joy is an indestructible joy. Secondly, we're to have an attitude of prayer. Regular, disciplined times of prayer are to be supplemented by a spirit of prayerfulness throughout the day, as we develop an increasingly automatic 'prayer reflex' whatever circumstances we might face. Thirdly, we're to have an attitude of gratitude. Thanklessness is a strange disorder for the Christian, which can only be explained by our forgetting Calvary. Sometimes circumstances make it hard for us to rejoice, but again the gospel itself is the key in the sense that ultimately the victory of the gospel overcomes every other defeat, and the joy of the gospel overcomes every other sorrow.

These, and many other commands like them scattered throughout the Scriptures, are the standing orders of the gospel. They are orders which Christ himself obeyed completely. He modelled joy in God, prayerful dependence on God and constant thankfulness to God. This was the will of God for him. This is the will of God for us in him.

Having laid out our standing orders, at verse 19 Paul adds the command: 'Do not quench the Spirit.' In the Bible, the work of the Holy Spirit is often pictured as a fire. Don't put out the fire, says Paul. Remember all that we saw about the work of the Holy Spirit in Chapter 5, and all that we saw about the implications of the completion of the Bible earlier in this chapter. To 'quench the Spirit' means refusing to hear and heed the truth which God has revealed. It happens when we ignore or downplay the significance of the Spirit-breathed word of God in the Scriptures. It happens when we fail to use the ordinary means of grace, given by God that his Spirit might do his work in us through his word. It happens when we take church attendance lightly. It happens when we know what is right and good, because it has been revealed to us in God's word, but we nonetheless follow after our own sinful ways. It happens when we take Jesus for granted.

So Paul's command today is simply this: submit completely to the word of God so that you come to know, love and serve the Lord Jesus more and more. As you do so, the Spirit of God will do his work within you, and the flame of the Spirit will burn brightly in your life.

Obedience is the opener of eyes

That takes us a step deeper into the Bible's teaching on guidance. From here we're going to turn for help to Romans 12:1-2. You may be aware that Romans is one of the most extended explanations of the gospel in the whole Bible. Paul spends eleven chapters explaining what God has done to save sinners. From the beginning of chapter twelve, he then turns to apply the implications of the gospel to our practical living. His aim is that we might be able to 'discern what is the will of God, what is good and acceptable and perfect' (verse 2). So it's interesting that the first thing he does is to urge Christians, in response to the gospel, to 'present your bodies as a living sacrifice, holy and acceptable to God' (verse 1). Total surrender in obedient service to God is one of the keys to discerning his will. George MacDonald, who was a huge influence on C. S. Lewis, said that 'Obedience is the opener of eyes.'[2] In other words, rather than seeking to deepen our understanding in order to obey, we need to obey what we know in order to be led into deeper understanding and deeper obedience. 'By obeying one learns to obey.'[3]

This means that, before we even know where God will lead us in our lives, we need to have made a prior decision that we will surrender to him. The point of a sacrifice in the Old Testament was that it was offered up wholly to God. Paul tells us that we are to be 'living sacrifices', offered up to God in a whole-of-life worship that holds nothing back. The more we do this, the better we will understand God's guidance for our lives.

The transformation we need

From here we move into an important theme which is really the deepest and most important answer to the question of divine guidance. Paul says in verse 2 that, having once lived our lives *conformed* to the ways of this world, we are to be *transformed* by the renewing of our minds, so that we are ultimately *reformed* to discern and delight in God's will.

Paul knows that the unbelieving world teaches us to think and act selfishly, and even as he writes to Christians he has to urge them (as J. B. Phillips famously translated verse 2) to not let the world 'squeeze you into its mould'. The world has a way of thinking about life and setting priorities. It lives for certain things, values certain things, dismisses certain things. It assesses the value of people in certain ways. And it wants you to fall into line.

I hope you can see that this goes far deeper than just maintaining certain times in our lives, or certain areas, or certain aspects, where we give God control. We give him Sundays, and the prayer meeting, a quiet time, and some of our money, and then we consider ourselves to be 'living as Christians'. Paul is saying that, as Christians who

[2] C. S. Lewis, *George Macdonald: An Anthology* (London: Geoffrey Bles, 1946), p. 42.
[3] *Ibid.*, p. 118.

are going to church and avoiding obvious immorality and doing religious things, it is perfectly possible for us nevertheless to be living our whole lives within a framework and a mentality which has not been set by God, but by this present evil age.

There's a story of a man called Petrov, who was a prisoner in a Soviet gulag. Every day Petrov went to work in a designated area, and every night he would come back to the camp and pass through a checkpoint. He returned one night with a wheelbarrow containing a sack. The checkpoint guard searched through the sack, but found nothing but sawdust. The next day, the same thing happened. The guard was convinced that Petrov was stealing something and so he plied him with questions. He searched through the sack, he emptied it out, but again there was nothing but sawdust. After a while the guard became so exasperated that he pleaded with Petrov to tell him what he was stealing, and promised not to inform on him. Petrov said, 'Wheelbarrows, sir, I am stealing wheelbarrows.'[4]

Sometimes the problem is not the individual things that happen *within* our lives, but that the *entire framework* of our lives has been based upon the world's thinking. We use the right language, do the right things and stand up for Christian values; but somehow we miss the fact that, through it all, our whole underlying understanding of life has been taken from the world and not from the word. In practical terms, we order our lives like anyone else: we see what job we can get with the best salary and conditions, we then decide which part of town we'd like to live in and what house we can afford, and we then think about what car we'd like to drive. Then we'll maybe start to wonder if there are any gospel-focused churches nearby, if the demands of work will leave us any time for fellowship with other Christians, and if the demands of our lifestyle will leave us any money to give to the church. We may be living

---

[4] William Edgar, 'Worship in All of Life', in *Give Praise to God*, ed. Philip Ryken, Derek Thomas and J. Ligon Duncan III (Phillipsburg: Presbyterian & Reformed, 2003), pp. 346-7.

outwardly obedient lives, in the sense of avoiding obvious sins, but our whole approach to life has been shaped without reference to God. We believe in him, but our commitment to him has to fit within a framework of life which has been set by the world. We inspect the sawdust carefully, but through goes the wheelbarrow.

Therefore, says Paul, we need to be transformed. Our minds need to be renewed. This is a deep work of God, carried out not merely at the level of the brain but throughout the whole person. Our thinking, attitudes and desires need to be changed. Our mindset needs to change, so that our minds are brought into line with God's. It is then that we'll be able to discern his will and see the goodness of his ways.

Paul describes the same process in Ephesians 4:22-24, where he says that Christians were taught

> to put off your old self, which belongs to your former manner of life and is corrupt through deceitful desires, and to be renewed in the spirit of your minds, and to put on the new self, created after the likeness of God in true righteousness and holiness.

God's work in the gospel is not only to forgive us our sins so that we can go to heaven, but to make us new here and now. He does that by renewing us after his own likeness. To say the same thing another way, he makes us more and more like Jesus.

I no longer live...

This is the key to guidance in the Christian life. It's not about a weird, mystical process of emptying your mind and waiting to hear a voice speaking to you. If you do that, then I suppose whatever you hear inside could be the Holy Spirit; but it seems to me it could equally be the voice of your own ego, or of Satan, or of indigestion. How will you know? Neither does God guide us by having us compile a database of Biblical rules for specific decisions. Instead he nurtures Christ-like character in us, forming it by the work of the Holy Spirit, helping us to make all our decisions in good and

God-honouring ways. After all, Christ is the supreme example of one who perfectly discerned and delighted in the will of the Father. He was fully aligned to the Father's mind, and lived to please him.

This means that the real key to understanding how God guides us in our lives is Christlikeness. Our deepest understanding of God's will and ways comes about through a growing relationship with him. Let me illustrate this by way of contrast. Many years ago I studied law, and I vividly remember studying for my criminal law exam. I had to memorise about eight hundred cases. I had to know the name of the case, what it was about, the court's decision, and what its significance was for later cases. So there I sat at my desk, drinking deeply unhealthy quantities of coffee and trying to cram all this information into my unwilling mind.

Compare that with another picture. Imagine a married couple. They have been together for many years, and are deeply in love. When they first married, they would both say and do things which were hurtful and irritating to one another; but now, many years down the line, this man and woman have become attuned to one another in a wonderful way. They instinctively sense one another's desires and respond accordingly. They know what will be pleasing or upsetting to the other, and care deeply about it. In a sense their minds, and even their desires, have become aligned so that they intuitively understand one another. Each can anticipate what will please the other, even without having to be told.

Making decisions which please the Lord is much more like the second of these pictures than the first. We get to know him better, we come to love him more and more, and over time as we become more like Jesus we develop a God-honouring instinct. Our minds are renewed after his likeness, realigned and recalibrated against his mind so that we can weigh his will and sense what is pleasing to him. As we draw closer to the Lord, we develop an intuitive sense of what pleases him. In a genuinely breathtaking phrase, Paul told the Galatian church that for their sake he was in the pains of childbirth 'until Christ is formed in you' (Galatians 4:19). In the same letter he described what it means to have the mind of Christ formed in us:

> I have been crucified with Christ. It is no longer I who live, but Christ who lives in me. And the life I now live in the flesh I live by faith in the Son of God, who loved me and gave himself for me. (Galatians 2:20)

Can you see why I said earlier that God guides us in ways which are far more wonderful than messages which are written across the sky? As he makes us more and more like Christ, we are helped to discern 'what is good and acceptable and perfect', which is how Paul defines 'the will of God' in Romans 12:2. A greater likeness to Christ helps us to recognise and approve whatever is like him, and conversely to recognise and reject whatever is unlike him.

This takes us back to the basic things of the Christian faith, which is good news because it's refreshingly down-to-earth and because it places all Christians on a level playing field. By constantly seeking to know Christ better, reading our Bibles, going to church, enjoying Christian fellowship, working hard to develop a disciplined prayer life, and receiving the sacraments, we can grow more like Christ and so make better decisions every day. Consider, for example, the fruit of the Spirit: love, joy, peace, patience, kindness, goodness, faithfulness, gentleness, self-control. If the Holy Spirit is producing this kind of character and life in us, so that we display this fruit in increasing abundance, will we not be guided into good and God-honouring decision-making?

Conclusion: the main things

Someone has said that the Christian life is about getting the main things right most of the time. We are to repent of our sins, trust in Jesus, walk in close fellowship with God, pursue Christ-like character, and seek the glory of God in all things. We are to obey his will in the specific commands that he has given, and we're to ask him for wisdom to discern and delight in his will in all things. Having done that, don't spend your life second-guessing every decision you make, or worrying that it might place you outside the will of God for you. That will only tie you in knots. If, on the other hand, you focus on making good and godly decisions which honour Christ and glorify God, that will set you free.

CHAPTER NINE

Following Jesus in Our Love for Others: The Essentials of Relationships

Or do you not know that the unrighteous will not inherit the kingdom of God? Do not be deceived: neither the sexually immoral, nor idolaters, nor adulterers, nor men who practise homosexuality, [10] nor thieves, nor the greedy, nor drunkards, nor revilers, nor swindlers will inherit the kingdom of God. [11] And such were some of you. But you were washed, you were sanctified, you were justified in the name of the Lord Jesus Christ and by the Spirit of our God.

[12] 'All things are lawful for me', but not all things are helpful. 'All things are lawful for me', but I will not be enslaved by anything. [13] 'Food is meant for the stomach and the stomach for food'—and God will destroy both one and the other. The body is not meant for sexual immorality, but for the Lord, and the Lord for the body. [14] And God raised the Lord and will also raise us up by his power. [15] Do you not know that your bodies are members of Christ? Shall I then take the members of Christ and make them members of a prostitute? Never! [16] Or do you not know that he who is joined to a prostitute becomes one body with her? For, as it is written, 'The two will become one flesh.' [17] But he who is joined to the Lord becomes one spirit with him. [18] Flee from sexual immorality. Every other sin a person commits is outside the body, but the sexually immoral person sins against his own body. [19] Or do you not know that your body is a temple of the Holy Spirit within you, whom you have from God? You are not your own, [20] for you were bought with a price. So glorify God in your body.

> *¹ Now concerning the matters about which you wrote: 'It is good for a man not to have sexual relations with a woman.' ² But because of the temptation to sexual immorality, each man should have his own wife and each woman her own husband. ³ The husband should give to his wife her conjugal rights, and likewise the wife to her husband. ⁴ For the wife does not have authority over her own body, but the husband does. Likewise the husband does not have authority over his own body, but the wife does. ⁵ Do not deprive one another, except perhaps by agreement for a limited time, that you may devote yourselves to prayer; but then come together again, so that Satan may not tempt you because of your lack of self-control.* – 1 Corinthians 6:9–7:5.

Introduction: the dvu of God

Wycliffe Bible translators were once working in Cameroon to translate the Bible into the Mbam cluster of languages. Working with the Hdi people, a language group which has about thirty thousand speakers, translators called Lee and Tammi Bramlett were pondering the Hdi word for love. They knew that almost every verb in the language had forms ending with the letters *-i*, *-a* and *-u*, and that the different forms were used in different ways. They also realised that they had only ever come across the Hdi word for love in two of the three forms: *dvi* and *dva*. So they gathered the translation committee, which included many influential members of the community.

'Could you *dvi* your wife?' they asked. The committee all agreed that you could. That would mean that the wife had been loved, but the love was gone.

The translators persisted: 'Could you *dva* your wife?' Again they agreed that you could, and this time explained that this love would depend on your wife's actions. As long as she remained a faithful wife and looked after her husband well, she would be loved.

They then asked, 'Could you *dvu* your wife?' The committee laughed. This was preposterous. They explained that this would mean you would have to continue loving your wife no matter what she did. Even if she failed to care for you, or cook for you, or even if she committed adultery with another man, you would have to continue loving her. They would never use the word in that way.

One of the translators sat for a moment and then asked quietly, 'Could God *dvu* people?' There was total silence, and then the members of the committee, who were mostly elderly men, began to weep.

> Do you know what this would mean? This would mean that God kept loving us over and over, millennia after millennia, while all that time we rejected his great love. He is compelled to love us, even though we have sinned more than any people.

So it was that this people came to see for the first time that God loves us, not because we are lovable, but because he is Love. In response to that breakthrough, the number of believers in that people group grew from a few hundred to several thousand. Today the word of God declares to this people the amazing news that God so *dvu'd* the world that he gave his Son so that those who believe in him might live.[1]

The character of God's love for us is the starting-point for our thinking about how we as disciples of Jesus are called to love others. The topic of relationships is a very broad one, but here we're going to focus on what the Bible has to say about dating, marriage and sex. How should followers of Jesus think and act in these areas? How does the gospel impact these things? And if being a Christian means loving and following Jesus in everything, how do we make sure that we do that first and foremost, even as we go about the business of loving others? Our aim here is not to mine the Bible for individual verses that give simple answers to these questions, but to rather start to *think like the Bible*, so that we can truly understand what love

---

[1] Bob Creson, 'God so "dvu"-d the world…', http://www.wycliffe.net/articles?id=2922&continent=AFR&country=CM. Accessed 18 April 2018.

looks like and why. When we do that, we discover that our love for others needs to look upward, outward and forward.

Love that looks upward

The lesson we learned from the Hdi people is that we need to look upwards in order to understand and experience the true character of God's love for us, so that this then shapes the way we love others. The apostle John was known as 'the apostle of love', as he repeatedly emphasised the command that Christians should love one another. When he wrote to believers to encourage them in that, he summarised the foundation of all that he wrote in three words: 'God is love' (1 John 4:8). That's not to say that God is defined by love, as if love is *all* that he is, but rather that love is defined by reference to God. All other love is only really love to the extent that it is like the love which is inherent in God's character.

So we look upwards to see what love is really like, and what we find is something that immediately challenges everything we hear in our culture. From our movies, magazines and soap operas you would think that true love is nothing more than an intense feeling that comes and goes with mood and circumstance. We fall into it, and we fall out of it. Most of the time, it is spoken of as something that *happens to us*. Love is some kind of mysterious power, rendering us helpless before its demands, and making us slaves to the feelings that arise within us. We insist we have to 'follow our hearts', even if that means breaking our promises. We act as if we're astonished that our feelings don't remain exactly the same for decades on end, and as if this gives us good reason to cast aside our commitments and responsibilities. We speak as if falling in love with someone who is not our spouse was perhaps regrettable in some ways, but undeniable and irresistible. 'It just happened.' This is just selfishness dressed up in the language of love, and it leaves a trail of misery in its wake.

In contrast, what do we find when we look upwards, to the love of God? In the Bible's storyline, God chooses a people and binds himself to them through something called a *covenant*. A covenant is not just a contract, but a gracious and binding commitment of life and soul. God says, 'I will be your God, and you will be my people, come what may.' The sheer strength and glory of that covenant commitment of love is seen most fully in the gospel. Listen to what John says in his first letter:

> Anyone who does not love does not know God, because God is love. In this the love of God was made manifest among us, that God sent his only Son into the world, so that we might live through him. In this is love, not that we have loved God but that he loved us and sent his Son to be the propitiation[2] for our sins. Beloved, if God so loved us, we also ought to love one another. No one has ever seen God; if we love one another, God abides in us and his love is perfected in us (1 John 4:8-12).

When John says that God 'so loved us' (verse 12), he doesn't mean 'so much' but 'in this way'. In other words, the *character* of God's love for us as a gracious, undeserved love should serve as the model for our love for others. Thus the gospel shows us how to love one another. In this, as in every area of Christian discipleship, the gospel itself must shape our lives.

So what does the gospel tell us about the nature of love? It tells us that real love is a rock-solid commitment to the eternal joy of the beloved. It tells us that real love is willing to suffer and sacrifice – to bleed and die – for the sake of the beloved. It tells us that real love is not conditional on being earned or deserved but is freely given, and continues to be given even when it's hard. It tells us that real love is faithful and true, and that it always keeps its promises. It tells us that love is patient and kind, it does not envy or boast, it is not arrogant or rude, it is not self-serving or irritable or resentful, it does not rejoice in wrongdoing but instead rejoices in the truth. It bears

[2] Or, in others words, an atoning sacrifice.

all things, and believes all things, and hopes all things, and endures all things. It never ends (1 Cor. 13).

Real love is something very different from what our culture has told us – not less but far, far more. It's richer, deeper and better in every way. The love shared between a man and a woman is intended to reflect the love that God has for us. In fact, Paul insists that Christian marriage is a picture, or a presentation, of the gospel itself (Ephesians 5:22-33). In these verses Paul notes that in a Christian marriage, a husband is to love his wife as Christ loved the church and gave himself for her, and a wife is to love her husband as the church loves Christ. In this way, marriage becomes 'a platform displaying God's glory' to the world.[3]

So love looks upward in the sense that it takes its nature and character from the love that God has for us. But love also looks upward in another sense, looking to God for his guidance and direction. In practice that means looking down, at our Bibles, to see what God has told us about his design for sexuality. This is crucial to every Christian discussion of sex and relationships. God created us with a physical and emotional design which we ignore at our peril. His instructions about relationships are not given to stifle us, but to liberate and enable us to be who he made us to be. They're not there because sex is something dirty that God wants us to avoid, but because sex is something wonderful that God wants us to enjoy. Contrary to popular perception, the Bible is stunningly positive in its teaching on sex. A whole book of the Bible, the Song of Songs, is (among other things) a surprisingly frank celebration of the sexual expression of true love. God gives sex as a wonderful gift. He also tells us how to ensure that, rather than being the utterly selfish pursuit it has so often become, it remains the mutually fulfilling and enriching thing that he created it to be. Enjoyed by God's design,

[3] Raymond C. Ortlund, 'Male-Female Equality and Male Headship: Genesis 1-3' in *Recovering Biblical Manhood and Womanhood*, ed. John Piper and Wayne Grudem, (Wheaton: Crossway, 1991), p. 102.

sex gives satisfaction in body and soul, binding us in joyful security to the one we love.

This applies to all people, believers or not, because it's simply the way God has created us. However, I also hope it's particularly obvious to you by now that Christians are not free to disregard the word of God. We don't have space here to go into the many complexities which surround this area, but the heart of the Bible's teaching is this: sex is a wonderful gift of God, given to be enjoyed only in the context of a lifelong, binding commitment of marriage between one man and one woman. Sexual expression outside of those boundaries goes against God's will for us, not because he hates us but because he loves us. If you read 1 Corinthians 6:9–7:5, it should be clear to you that the reason we shouldn't treat sex casually is because it's a precious gift of God.

The Bible's understanding of sexual expression has various consequences, and we should not be embarrassed to state them. Sexual activity separated from a true relationship, such as casual sex or the use of pornography, is wrong. Sexual activity between more than two people is wrong. 'Open' relationships, involving so-called sexual freedom, are wrong. Sexual activity between two men, or between two women, is wrong. Same-sex marriage is wrong. All sexual activity outside of marriage as the Bible defines it is wrong. And the reason for all of this is because God loves us so much.

Western culture has decisively rejected God's purposes and set its own course in these matters. This is immensely sad because of the damage it inflicts upon men, women and children, but in another sense it should be no surprise to us when a sinful culture embraces and even celebrates sin. What is even more tragic is that many churches are buckling under the cultural pressure and pretending that the Bible doesn't say what it clearly says about sex and marriage. Increasingly, the world stands in desperate need of a clear witness to God's design for human sexuality. Our culture might *declare* that it has achieved liberation in these things, but what it displays is an immeasurable avalanche of pain and misery arising from broken relationships. Let me say it again: the reason God hates that, and longs to see strong families bound together in covenant love, is because he loves us so much. In such a culture, what an opportunity we have today, as disciples of Jesus, to model something different and better.

Let me say clearly that if you're involved in a sexual lifestyle which you know to be contrary to God's will, you need to stop it immediately. This is too important to be coy about, because such a lifestyle does terrible relational and spiritual damage. If you're a new Christian it may be that you had no idea that your behaviour was sinful, but now you know. Your conversion may raise all manner of difficult and complex practical issues about your life and relationships, but it's crucial that you remember the depth of God's love for you. As you have trusted him to forgive your sins and give you new life, trust him to guide your life now. It's imperative that you address these things urgently in repentance and faith. You will need the love and support of other Christians as you seek to pursue holiness, so speak to your pastor about this. Helpfully, there is an increasing array of excellent resources to help Christians to respond well to these issues.[4]

In thinking about our relationships, we need to begin by looking upward.

Love that looks outward

The next stage which naturally follows is that love looks outward. Much that passes for love in our culture is essentially selfishness. It's about my needs being met, my happiness being served and my agenda being pursued. If I'm not happy any more, I'm within my rights to leave. If I believe I could be happier with someone else, I'm within my rights to leave. In fact – people really do say this kind of

---

[4] See for example Rosaria Butterfield, *The Secret Thoughts of an Unlikely Convert* (Pittsburgh: Crown & Covenant, 2012).

thing – to stay with the one I promised to love for ever would be 'untrue to myself'. In a supreme proof of the self-deceiving power of sin, people manage to conclude that keeping their promises would make them untrue to themselves!

The love that we see in the gospel, and see commended in God's word, is love that looks outwards. It's not focussed on self, but on the beloved. In fact, it involves a genuine surrender of self. Do you remember the traditional marriage vow? 'With my body I honour you, all that I am I give to you, all that I have I share with you.'

One of the most moving books I have ever read was written by a man called J. Robertson McQuilkin. He was president of a Bible college in America, and spoke all over the world, but his wife Muriel began to show signs of Alzheimer's disease. Eventually he concluded that 'it has become apparent that Muriel is contented most of the time she is with me and almost none of the time I am away from her… it is clear to me that she needs me now, full-time'.[5] Robertson spoke of how the decision to give up the Bible college presidency was made forty-two years earlier, when he promised to care for her in sickness and in health. 'I don't *have* to care for her,' he insisted, 'I get to! It is a high honour to care for so wonderful a person.'[6]

McQuilkin tells the story of a simple incident:

> Once our flight was delayed in Atlanta and we had to wait a couple of hours. Now that's a challenge. Every few minutes, the same questions, the same answers about what we're doing here, when are we going home? And every few minutes we'd take a fast-paced walk down the terminal in earnest search of – what? Muriel had always been a speed walker. I had to jog to keep up with her!
>
> An attractive woman executive type sat across from us, working diligently on her computer. Once, when we returned from an excursion, she said something, without looking up from her papers. Since no one else was nearby I assumed she had spoken to me or at least mumbled in protest of our constant activity.

[5] J. Robertson McQuilkin, *A Promise Kept* (Carol Stream: Tyndale House, 2006), pp. 21-22.
[6] *Ibid.*, p. 23.

'Pardon?' I asked.

'Oh,' she said, 'I was just asking myself, "Will I ever find a man to love me like that?"'[7]

The book is called *A Promise Kept*. McQuilkin is a man who understood marriage. I promised. Circumstances may have changed, and life may not be what I thought it would be, but I promised.

Jesus did not say to us: I will love you as long as you return my love to a satisfactory standard, or as long as I find it fulfilling, or as long as it makes me happy, or unless this causes me great pain. He said: I will love you if it kills me; if it strips me of everything that is mine; if it causes me anguish of body and soul that you could never comprehend; if it drives nails through my hands and feet, and leaves me gasping for breath and screaming in pain. I will love you.

It is the glory of the marriage vow that it reflects this limitless commitment of love. A man and woman, entering into the marriage covenant as God intended, know from that moment that their spouse will be with them and for them forever, bound by law, honour and covenant. This commitment will remain, no matter what. Marriage looks at every possible calamity that could befall a man and wife, and with eyes wide open it says, 'all that I am I give to you… for better, for worse… for richer, for poorer… in sickness and in health… until death…'.

It should be obvious that marriage, even between two Christians, is going to bring very significant challenges. Marriage takes one sinner and puts him together with another sinner to share everything in life, for the rest of their lives. In the normal course of things they will likely bring other little sinners into the world too, to be raised by the two sinners we already had. Why would we assume that it is going to be an idyllic scenario? It will bring immense challenges and frustrations, but again, those are played out against the backdrop of a permanent commitment in which the possibility of separation is

[7] J. Robertson McQuilkin, *A Promise Kept*, pp. 18-19.

never contemplated. The permanence and sacredness of the bond is the unique glory of marriage.

It's also this unique glory of marriage that explains why God has given sex as a gift to be enjoyed only in that context. Sex involves a total physical surrender of yourself to another, with nothing held back. It's a supremely vulnerable act, and it is simply wrong to ask of someone a total commitment of body while refusing to give them a total commitment of life. Sex outside of marriage says to someone, in effect, that you want their body but you're not willing to commit to them wholeheartedly. You want them to give you sexual pleasure, but you're not willing to give them the security within which such total surrender is safe. You're not willing to guarantee that you won't walk away.

The world, of course, will scoff. Unbelievers, and sadly sometimes even ill-informed believers, will insist that they can be committed to someone without being married to them. It's not true. You can only *feel* committed to them, which is a very different thing. The point is that marriage is the commitment. Marriage is the public, legally binding union of a man and a woman, not in a contract (valid as long as we decide) but in a covenant (binding forever). When you have a sexual relationship with someone to whom you're not married, you can pack your bags and leave any time you like.

God knows, as our Creator, that total physical surrender to another person requires total commitment of life to that person. This is why he asks and commands that, as we love others, we do so with a love that looks outward.

Love that looks forward

Finally, it's important to add that love looks forward. Eternity stretches before us, and we should have no desire to be married to someone who (as far as we can know) will be spending it in a different place from us. The biblical pattern for marriage is that believers should marry believers. For a Christian knowingly to marry an unbeliever is not only unwise but wrong. This is an issue which Christians sometimes struggle with, but it's so important that I've included a separate appendix (Appendix 1) explaining the Bible's teaching in this area.

Of course, it's perfectly possible that you have come to faith after your marriage. In that case you will need great wisdom and grace, and unceasing prayer, to seek the salvation of your unbelieving spouse and children. If the gospel is true, there can be nothing more important to you now than your loved ones coming to have a living faith in Christ and so inherit eternal life.

If on the other hand you are a single Christian who would love to be married, let me encourage you not to give up in your faith-fulness to God's pattern. Don't give in to the temptation to cast the net wider. Don't give in to the notion that you can start dating an unbeliever and they might then come to faith. If God had intended dating as a method of evangelism, he would have told us. I know that singleness is not an issue for some, and is an issue of enormous sorrow for others, but this is too important to act carelessly. Tim and Kathy Keller have been counselling couples for over thirty years, and the temptation to marry an unbeliever is one of the most common issues they have faced in that time. They've also counselled countless couples who have gone ahead and done it. This is Kathy Keller's summary of what such Christians have experienced:

> 1. In order to be more in sync with your spouse, the Christian will have to push Christ to the margins of his or her life. This may not involve actually repudiating the faith, but in matters such as devotional life, hospitality to believers, missionary support, tithing, raising children in the faith, fellowship with other believers – those things will have to be minimized or avoided in order to preserve peace in the home.
>
> 2. Alternatively, if the believer in the marriage holds on to a robust Christian life and practice, the non-believing partner will have to be marginalized. If he or she can't understand the point of

Bible study and prayer, or missions trips, or hospitality, then he or she can't or won't participate alongside the believing spouse in those activities. The deep unity and oneness of a marriage cannot flourish when one partner cannot fully participate in the other person's most important commitments.

3. So either the marriage experiences stress and breaks up; or it experiences stress and stays together, achieving some kind of truce that involves one spouse or the other capitulating in some areas, but which leaves both parties feeling lonely and unhappy.[8]

Her article is an extended and heartfelt plea: Don't do it. Love looks forward.

Conclusion: redeemed for holiness

There is one final thing I need to say before closing this chapter. Many of us, reading this, are looking back on relationships which in one way or another have not followed God's design. In truth, all of us are. So if this applies to you, and you know that your past includes sexual sin, what does God say to you?

He says that you are his precious child. He says that he sent his Son to die for these sins of yours. He says that the blood of Jesus cleanses you from all unrighteousness. He says that your salvation is all of grace, and not of works. Consider again what Paul says in 1 Corinthians 6. He gives quite a list, mentioning the sexually immoral, idolaters, adulterers, those who practise homosexuality, thieves, the greedy, drunkards, revilers and swindlers. And, he says, 'such were some of you'.

> But you were washed, you were sanctified, you were justified in the name of the Lord Jesus Christ and by the Spirit of our God (1 Corinthians 6:11).

God has dealt with your past, so you can let go of it and know complete freedom. The consequences of past sin might linger, but by his

---

[8] Kathy Keller, 'Don't Take It from Me: Reasons You Should Not Marry an Unbeliever', https://www.thegospelcoalition.org/article/dont-take-it-from-me-reasons-you-should-not-marry-an-unbeliever. Accessed 18 April 2018.

grace the condemnation of it does not. Today you stand as a new creation in him, redeemed for holiness. So from this point forward, be who you are.

CHAPTER TEN

Following Jesus Through the Generations: The Essentials of Parenting

Children, obey your parents in the Lord, for this is right. ² 'Honour your father and mother' (this is the first commandment with a promise), ³ 'that it may go well with you and that you may live long in the land.' ⁴ Fathers, do not provoke your children to anger, but bring them up in the discipline and instruction of the Lord.
— Ephesians 6:1-4.

Introduction: why may not I?

John G. Paton was a missionary to the islands of the New Hebrides in the South Pacific. He was born in 1824 and raised in the south-west of Scotland, and in his extraordinary autobiography he describes the impact that his father's life and faith had upon him from his earliest years. The little cottage in which they lived had three rooms. One served as kitchen, living area and bedroom. Another was the workshop where Paton's father earned a living by manufacturing women's stockings. Between them was a final, small room which the family knew as 'the closet'.

> This was the Sanctuary of that cottage home. Thither daily, and oftentimes a day, generally after each meal, we saw our father retire, and 'shut to the door'; and we children got to understand by a sort of spiritual instinct (for the thing was too sacred to be talked about) that prayers were being poured out there for us, as

of old by the High Priest within the veil in the Most Holy Place. We occasionally heard the pathetic echoes of a trembling voice pleading as if for life, and we learned to slip out and in past that door on tiptoe, not to disturb the holy colloquy.

What impact did the knowledge of this praying father make upon the young James Paton?

> Never, in temple or cathedral, on mountain or in glen, can I hope to feel that the Lord God is more near, more visibly walking and talking with men, that under that humble cottage roof of thatch and oaken wattles. Though everything else in religion were by some unthinkable catastrophe to be swept out of memory, or blotted from my understanding, my soul would wander back to those early scenes, and shut itself up once again in that sanctuary closet, and, hearing still the echoes of those cries to God, would hurl back all doubt with the victorious appeal, 'He walked with God, why may not I?'[1]

There are millions of Christians who, under God, owe their introduction to Jesus to godly parents who spoke the gospel to them and lived the gospel before them. That may or may not have been your experience, but if you have children, you should long that it might be theirs.

I need to say something about the purpose and scope of this chapter. This is not a parenting manual, or a compendium of handy hints for mealtimes, bath-times and bedtimes. Our purpose here is much more basic, but foundational to all the practicalities of parenting. What we're aiming for here is clarity about the underlying principles and priorities that should govern our parenting. Only if we're clear what our ultimate aims are in parenting can we find help in the day-to-day practicalities.

When Paul wrote to the Christians in Ephesus, he addressed the issue of how parents and children should relate to one another, but he did so in the course of four verses. It's all very brief, and for some

---

[1] John G. Paton, *The Autobiography of the Pioneer Missionary to the New Hebrides: (Vanuatu)* (Edinburgh: Banner of Truth Trust, 2016), p. 8.

people that's a great frustration. Why couldn't Paul have told us more? The raising of family is a huge part of life. At certain points it can feel all-consuming. Why doesn't Paul give us more guidance? The reason, I think, is that he doesn't want to give us rules; he wants to give us the gospel. Sometimes people want to treat the Bible as if it is a manual of useful advice for life, a useful record of the accumulated wisdom of the ages. Some would have preferred it to be arranged thematically, so we could simply look up a topic and find the answers. There's no shortage of sermons out there on 'six steps to a happier family' or 'four principles for practical parenting', but the Bible doesn't work that way. The desire that it should is part of something called 'just-tell-me-what-to-do' syndrome. Don't put me to the hard work of letting the gospel sink deep into my soul. Don't expect me to work through the implications of grace-shaped living in a world that can be cruel, hurtful and just too busy. Don't ask me for the lifelong commitment and endurance of Christian faith. Just-tell-me-what-to-do! Give me a rule that I can obey. Give me a formula that I can follow.

In truth we should rejoice that God works the way he does, not merely imposing rules of behaviour upon us, but rather forming the character of Christ within us. That means we need to go beyond 'rules for parenting' and ask how the gospel affects family life. In fact, we need to go deeper still, and ask how family life can reflect and serve the gospel. If you're a parent, how can you ensure that your parenting will bring glory to God and serve the cause of his kingdom?

Long for your children to know and love Christ

The first step is to get our priorities right. I hope by this stage it isn't necessary for me to write this, but you need to long for your children to know and love Christ. I mention this because it never ceases to amaze me how many Christian parents will say something very similar to what non-Christian parents say all the time: 'I just want her to be healthy and happy.' Let me say it clearly: in a Christian, that is a sorry excuse for an ambition for your children. If all that you want for them is that they might be healthy and happy for a few years here on this earth, then you have not understood the gospel. If your deepest desire is that you might leave them an inheritance which can be measured in bank account balances and property, then you need to reconsider what is the greatest inheritance that parents can leave to their children.

Your children are a sacred trust. They belong to God more than they belong to you. He loves them more than you do, and he formed them for himself. He created them, with their individual circumstances and personalities, to know infinite joy in knowing him for all eternity. He has placed them under your care that you might raise them to trust in him, for God's glory and for their joy. If by some turn of events you had to choose between the earthly health and happiness of your children and their eternal destiny, you should unhesitatingly choose eternity. In the end, this world's treasures and pleasures are small, passing things when compared to what God has prepared for those who love him. As Scripture says eye has not seen, nor ear heard, nor the heart of man imagined the glories of the life to come (1 Corinthians 2:9).

For this reason it's important to remember that your children, while they are entrusted to you for a time, belong to God. When John Paton's parents heard that he wanted to serve as a missionary on the other side of the world, their response was 'that they had long since given me away to the Lord, and in this matter also would leave me to God's disposal'.[2]

As a Christian parent, then, one of your deepest longings in life should be that your children might know and love the Lord. One of the most important practical results of this is prayer. The responsibility to pray for your children is a heavy one, and you should do it daily. Who can tell how many children have persevered in

---

[2] John G. Paton, *Autobiography*, p. 43.

faith because, under the sovereignty of God, their parents prayed for them earnestly from the beginning of their lives? Plead with the Lord for them. He is the perfect Father who loves to give good gifts to his children.

Teach your children to know and love Christ

Paul expects that Christian parents will go further than just *desiring* that their children might know and love Christ, and that they will actively teach their children to know and love Christ. Christians should raise their children 'in the discipline and instruction of the Lord' (Ephesians 6:4). As Dietrich Bonhoeffer put it, 'It is from God that parents receive their children, and it is to him that they should lead them.'[3] Notice that this is the responsibility of parents. It cannot be 'out-sourced' to pastors, Sunday schools, youth groups or anyone else. These things certainly have their place in supporting parents in the demanding task of raising their children in the faith. There's an old saying that it takes a village to raise a child, and in many ways it takes a church to raise a Christian. However, in a Christian family, the church's role is only ever a supporting one. The main responsibility falls to parents to ensure that *so far as it lies with them*, their children will grow up knowing of a Saviour who died for them and who lives for them and who loves them.

I cannot stress strongly enough that the main element in the discipline and instruction of our children, as exemplified by John Paton's father, is personal example. You cannot give to your children what you don't possess yourself, and so your own relationship with Christ is crucial not only for your sake, but for your children's sake. C. H. Spurgeon said that 'A man's life is always more forcible than his speech; when men take stock of him they reckon his deeds as pounds and his words as pence.'[4] Depending on where you're reading this, you may need to convert that into your local currency – but you get the point.

[3] Dietrich Bonhoeffer, *Letters and Papers from Prison* (London: Collins, 1959), p. 153.
[4] C. H. Spurgeon, *Lectures to My Students*, p. 270.

When practice and preaching diverge, people will always be more influenced by a man's practice than by his preaching. That applies even more forcibly to the influence that we exert on our families.

It's a strange paradox that one of the things your children most need to know is that there is someone else whom you love more than you love them. Communicated in the wrong way, that can crush a child. Communicated in the right way, it will make them *more* secure in your love rather than less. For your part, by loving Christ first, you will love your children not less, but more.

Having insisted that example is paramount, we must recognise that the 'discipline and instruction' which Paul refers to clearly involves telling as well as showing. Christian parents should be deliberate in teaching their children the Christian faith and leading them in living the Christian life. Worldly wisdom would say that we should do no such thing. According to many, we should raise our children in some kind of neutral atmosphere, allowing them to 'make up their own mind what they believe when they're old enough'. Of course our children must come to embrace their own faith, but this way of thinking is wrong for two main reasons. First, there is no such thing as a neutral upbringing: our lives declare to our children, loud and clear, either that God is real and important or that he is not. Secondly, the gospel is in fact true, and to do anything other than to commend it to our children in every possible way would be deeply unloving.

So we 'instruct' our children in what it means to be a Christian, and we 'discipline' them accordingly. Here we come to another important principle. We are to *discipline* our children because they are *disciples*. It's fascinating that Paul addresses himself directly to children in the early church (Ephesians 6:1-3; Colossians 3:20), treating them as members of the covenant community and as Christians with a distinctive response to make to the gospel. The children of believing people are in a uniquely privileged position, and we should be very wary about raising them as unbelievers in need of a conversion experience of some specific kind. Rather we should nurture them in faith from their earliest years, since the children of disciples are themselves disciples. Such a privilege was mine, with the result that I have no conversion experience to speak of. In fact, one of God's greatest gifts to me is a boring testimony! I cannot remember a time when I did not know that Jesus was real and the gospel was true. I had to grow into that faith, as I still do, but I was a part of Christ's church from the beginning of my life. Of course, some children will sadly walk away from the faith in which they are raised; but our default should be to treat them as disciples, and as members of the church, unless and until they remove themselves from that privilege.

What does all of this mean in practice? It means sharing with our children, regularly and deliberately, the kind of teaching that is set out in this book; setting a godly example day by day to them, and weaving faith into the normal rhythms of life; leading them in Bible study and prayer from their earliest years, so that as soon as they can understand anything, they know that Jesus loves them; applying the gospel to our lives, and to their lives, so that they can see the difference that being a Christian makes; and treasuring opportunities to grow in faith, since your children will most often come to value what you value.

In one of the most foundational texts in the Old Testament, we read this:

> Hear, O Israel: The LORD our God, the LORD is one. You shall love the LORD your God with all your heart and with all your soul and with all your might. And these words that I command you today shall be on your heart. You shall teach them diligently to your children, and shall talk of them when you sit in your house, and when you walk by the way, and when you lie down, and when you rise (Deuteronomy 6:4-7).

Moses goes on to explain to the people of Israel that, when their children ask the meaning of the Scriptures, they are to explain the great deliverance which the Lord brought about when he rescued his people from slavery in Egypt. In the same way, when the children of Christian parents ask why the family lives the way it does, this is an opportunity to explain to them the great redemption which Christ has purchased for his people, and the new life into which he has led them.

Teach your children to love Christ's church

There is one aspect of Christian nurture that is so important that I want to mention it separately. As Christians, we should teach our children to love Christ's church. There are many factors which will influence your children's spiritual wellbeing throughout their lives. One of the most significant will be the extent to which they become convinced of the need for a deep involvement with a specific, gospel-teaching, local church community. Like love for Jesus himself, love for his church is something which children will often 'catch' from their parents. It's one of the best infections you can pass on to them!

That means that church needs to be one of the regular rhythms of your family life. It should be a fixed anchor in the week, unmissable unless in extreme circumstances. Children attending church week by week, should see what it means to their parents that they are taught from the Bible, and are able to worship God in praise, and to share fellowship with God's people. Where parents are eager to be in church, and will rearrange other aspects of life accordingly, children pick up on this and instinctively understand that corporate worship is something glorious and important.

At the risk of stating the obvious, if it hasn't come already, the time will almost certainly come when your children will not want to attend church on a Sunday. It may be that they go through a stage where they question what they believe, but equally it may be something simpler. Where I serve, church clashes with sports, music, dancing and a host of other hobbies and interests which a secular culture now places before our children. I have become more and more convinced that the only wise course for Christian parents is to protect Sundays carefully, and especially to protect church attendance. It's very easy to find reasons to make exceptions, but when we do we are telling our children that other things, if they are exciting enough, are more important than meeting with God's people. This is not good or wise. It can feel as if strict enforcement of church attendance might turn our children away from church, and Christian parents often slacken the reins with the best of intentions, but experience suggests that the outcome is rarely good.

Instead, make church attendance the first commitment in the family's diary every week. Make sure, perhaps through hospitality in your home, that your children get to know not only other children in the church, but adults too. Make clear to them how much church means to you, and how essential it is in the whole pattern of how you follow Jesus. Where things go wrong in church, as they will do from time to time, be careful how you speak in front of your children. Negativity and cynicism are to be guarded against at all times, but they should never be expressed in front of our children.

Teach your children how to navigate a Christ-rejecting world

Finally, it is also important for Christian parents to teach their children how to navigate a Christ-rejecting world. At the most basic level, children will often need help to understand why most of their classmates don't love Jesus, or even mock them for their faith. More deeply, they will need to be protected from the many lies which the unbelieving world tells them every day. As I write, our children are increasingly being indoctrinated by our culture to think, speak and act in certain ways. The impact of this is very great. Once again, it is your responsibility as a parent to care for the spiritual wellbeing of your children. With great patience, care and wisdom, it will be necessary for you to educate your children in the many areas where the world is leading them astray.

In all of this there is a delicate balance between two extremes. Some children are left open to the influence of the unbelieving world far too much, and their thinking is shaped accordingly. Others are overly protected by their parents, from the best of motives, but then have no resources to cope when they reach the stage where they have to find their own place in the world. Christian parents need great wisdom to encourage their children towards adopting a Christian worldview and mindset.

Conclusion: the channels of grace

It's important, as we conclude this chapter, to remind ourselves that our children are ultimately in God's hands. Too many Christian parents have suffered under a crushing burden of guilt and failure. In spite of fervent prayer, they have seen their children drift from the faith which they had sought to nurture in them. What did I do? What did I fail to do? These are the anguished questions of many a Christian parent, as if there really was a formula for guaranteed success which everyone else knows about, but which they somehow missed. We must remember that our authority in parenting is an authority delegated by God, within limits. He gives us great responsibility and great privileges, but he does not make us sovereign over the lives of our children. He does not give us control. Recognising the sovereignty of God means recognising the Father who stands behind all fathers (and mothers).

In the face of the many mistakes we all make, our God offers forgiveness and new beginnings. We thank him for past joys, seek forgiveness for past wrongs, ask healing for past hurts, and look to him for grace that we might more and more become the parents he would have us be. Wonderfully, God uses us, in all our flawed parenting, to bring about his good purposes for our children. Dale Ralph Davis has a beautiful expression in one of his books, in his dedication to his parents:

I have always been grateful for them but even more so as the years wear on. I confess God's grace named my name before the foundation of the world (Eph. 1:3-6), but when he poured out that grace in time he made most of it flow through my parents.[5]

[5] Dale Ralph Davis, *2 Samuel: Out of Every Adversity* (Fearn, Ross-shire: Christian Focus, 1999), p. 7.

CHAPTER ELEVEN

Following Jesus in His World:
The Essentials of Evangelism

… but we endure anything rather than put an obstacle in the way of the gospel of Christ. [13] Do you not know that those who are employed in the temple service get their food from the temple, and those who serve at the altar share in the sacrificial offerings? [14] In the same way, the Lord commanded that those who proclaim the gospel should get their living by the gospel.

[15] But I have made no use of any of these rights, nor am I writing these things to secure any such provision. For I would rather die than have anyone deprive me of my ground for boasting. [16] For if I preach the gospel, that gives me no ground for boasting. For necessity is laid upon me. Woe to me if I do not preach the gospel! [17] For if I do this of my own will, I have a reward, but if not of my own will, I am still entrusted with a stewardship. [18] What then is my reward? That in my preaching I may present the gospel free of charge, so as not to make full use of my right in the gospel.

[19] For though I am free from all, I have made myself a servant to all, that I might win more of them. [20] To the Jews I became as a Jew, in order to win Jews. To those under the law I became as one under the law (though not being myself under the law) that I might win those under the law. [21] To those outside the law I became as one outside the law (not being outside the law of God but under the law of Christ) that I might win those outside the law. [22] To the weak I became weak, that I might win the weak.

I have become all things to all people, that by all means I might save some. ²³ I do it all for the sake of the gospel, that I may share with them in its blessings. – 1 Corinthians 9:12-23.

Introduction: I am sending you

In John 20, when Jesus appears to his disciples after his resurrection, he pronounces peace upon them. The very next thing he says is 'As the Father sent me, so I am sending you' (verse 21).

God the Son, sent by the Father, left the glories of heaven in order to seek and to save the lost. In that sense God is a 'going God': in Jesus, he goes to those who need him. God's people, in turn, are to be 'going people': we are those who have been sent by Christ to make him known. 'As the Father sent me, so I am sending you.' This is one of the main tasks which God has given to his church, and an important part of the calling of every disciple of Jesus. We follow Jesus in his world by obeying his command to make him known to others.

The earliest believers took that command with the utmost seriousness, and the book of Acts is the story of how Christ worked through them to build his church as he had promised he would do. It's a story of explosive growth. Acts tells us of the word of God increasing, and the number of the disciples multiplying, and the message of the gospel continuing to prevail mightily, and so on.

Every minister knows that there are two topics which make Christians break into a cold sweat. The first is prayer, and the second is evangelism. These are areas in which most believers feel entirely inadequate, and when we do, we've grasped exactly half of the truth. We *are* entirely inadequate in our own power. But the other half of the truth is that, when God asks us to do something for him, he always equips us with everything we need to do it. Without him we can do nothing (John 15:5); but it's also true that we can do all things through him who strengthens us (Philippians 4:13). That means the church's calling to mission – whether it's foreign missions ten thousand miles away, or personal evangelism in your own living room or workplace – is not something to fear. He calls every one of us, and he equips every one of us. The central question is whether we have confidence in the gospel itself.

There's an old story about an American shoe company which sent a salesman to a foreign country. He had hardly arrived when he cabled for money to come home. 'It's hopeless,' he reported. 'No one over here wears shoes.' The company brought him home, and sent another salesman over. This salesman immediately cabled back: 'Send me all the shoes you can make. The market is absolutely unlimited – no one here has shoes!'[1]

Our generation faces a stark choice when it comes to evangelism. The vast majority of people in the western world have no living faith in Jesus Christ, and no inkling that they need him. Many people do realise that they long for something more, but they're not breaking down the doors of the churches to find out about Jesus. If anything, our culture tends to mock Christian evangelism as ridiculous, or denounce it as offensive. We can respond in one of two ways. The first is to feel overwhelmed by it all. The ground is too hard and the task too hopeless. No one is interested. There's no point in telling people because no-one's listening. The alternative is to look at twenty-first century culture and say, 'Everyone here needs Jesus!' They may not know it, but that just means we need to start further back and be patient as we explain who he is, and why he's supremely important. We must remember, though, that the gospel is true and it is the deepest need of every man, woman and child on the face of the earth. We must also remember that the gospel is powerful, and that God is still in the business of seeking and saving the lost.

So as we consider the basics of evangelism, we are going to think about the why, the what, the who and the how.

---

[1] Dale Ralph Davis, *Joshua: No Falling Words* (Fearn, Ross-shire: Christian Focus, 2000), pp. 119-120.

The why: need and necessity

First we consider the *why* of mission: why is this so important? The ultimate reason, as with everything in life, is the glory of God. We exist to glorify him, and he is glorified as men and women are saved by his grace. But within that, the why of mission is *need and necessity*. Have a look at 1 Corinthians 9:12-23, and consider the sense of urgency that gripped Paul in his gospel work. He had a deep conviction that people need the gospel because, apart from Christ, they will eternally die. If that is not true, then we Christians are all fools. All the ministry and mission of our churches is a waste of time, money and effort. On the other hand, if it's true that we're all hurtling towards an eternity either with or without God, and that the difference is how we respond to Jesus Christ, there is nothing more important in the world than to make the gospel known. If we're not passionately longing for those we love to come to Christ, then we really haven't understood the gospel at all. There is a reason why Jesus walked deliberately to his death on the cross: it was the *only way* to accomplish his life's work to seek and to save the lost. It follows that the *only way* to be saved is to turn to him in faith, and so receive forgiveness and new life. We must confess our sin, repent of it, and seek forgiveness on the sole ground that Christ has died for us. That is the ultimate need of every human being.

This is why there is necessity placed upon us to make Christ known, which is how Paul puts it at verse 16: 'For necessity is laid upon me. Woe to me if I do not preach the gospel!'

Many years ago, I was happily practising as a civil litigator in the Scottish courts. It was an enjoyable and fulfilling career. But I was also reading John Stott's great book, *The Cross of Christ*, and one of the things the Lord used to call me to ministry was this inescapable sense of supreme necessity. The sheer truth and importance of the gospel so gripped my heart that I felt compelled to make it known. Woe to me if I failed to do so!

I don't want to suggest for a moment that if you're really serious about making the gospel known, you'll necessarily go into Christian ministry. That might apply to some, but my greatest hesitation in leaving the legal profession was my knowledge of how badly lawyers need the gospel! We need Christians in every walk of life, but we need them there with a sense of the necessity of making Christ known. Consider Paul's sense of urgency when he insists that 'we endure anything rather than put an obstacle in the way of the gospel of Christ' (1 Corinthians 9:12), or describes his willingness to 'become all things to all people, that by all means I might save some' (1 Corinthians 9:22). I will do anything, he says, to make the gospel known. This is how great the need is on the part of unsaved men and women. This is how great the necessity is on the part of God's people.

The what: gospel, gospel, gospel

If that's the *why*, what's the *what*? What should the content of our evangelism be? Paul's answer is very clear: it's gospel, gospel, gospel. This is unmistakable in the first part of the passage: in the space of seven verses, the word 'gospel' appears seven times. The gospel is what people need, and the gospel is what Paul feels compelled to preach.

This is the key to mission, and one of the main reasons why the mainline churches in the modern West have declined so catastrophically in the last half century. Huge swathes of the established churches have lost all confidence in the gospel. We don't like talking about sin, or mentioning the holiness and judgment of God, or suggesting that Jesus is the only way to be put right with God. We don't like talking about the need for repentance, and wholehearted commitment to Christ, and obedience to his word.

The problem is that, if you remove these things, you've lost the gospel. If there is no such problem as sin, then salvation is superfluous. If there's no judgment, it's unnecessary. If there are other ways to God, it's optional. There's certainly no urgent need to tell people about Jesus. If being a Christian is about being a nice person, then Jesus really has very little to do with it – there are millions of 'nice' people who don't believe in him. The church in our day has lost confidence in the essentials of the gospel, and as a result has completely lost its way because it doesn't know what it exists for. Our calling is to be ambassadors for Christ, taking his message to the world and imploring people to be reconciled to God through him (2 Corinthians 5:20).

The mission of the church is shaped by the gospel message, and by the need and necessity that so gripped Paul. If we are to communicate this to others, we need to be clear what the gospel is. We need to be clear, for example, that it's a message of good news. It's not good advice about how to get yourself right with God, but good news about how Jesus has made things right. It's not a demand to be obeyed, but a gift to be received. We also need to be clear that, although the gospel has huge lifestyle implications, the gospel is not primarily a lifestyle. You're not a Christian because you go to a church or live a moral life.

A Christian is someone who trusts in Jesus Christ, and so believes the gospel. The gospel is difficult to summarise in a few words because it's a diamond with many facets, but at its core is the glorious good news that although we are sinners who have rebelled against our Creator, Jesus died for our sins, and he rose again, and he is Lord. Jesus took in himself the death that we deserve for our rebellion against God. He then rose to a new, perfect and never-ending life, and he invites us into that life. Right now, he will put that life within us if we turn to him in faith, so that we have a new life to live now, and a perfect life to enjoy eternally.

This is the message God's people have been commissioned to proclaim. Where that is absent, or unclear, or even just assumed but never stated, the church loses all sense of what it exists for. It loses its sense of mission, and it inevitably declines.

The who: nations and neighbours

So there's a desperate need for the gospel to go out, but to whom are we to take it?

1. The nations

From the beginning, the programme was that the message of the gospel would be made known in Jerusalem, and then in the surrounding regions of Judea and Samaria, and then to the ends of the earth (Acts 1:8). If the gospel is the deepest need of every man, woman and child on the face of the earth, that means that it needs to go everywhere. It needs to go to the nations.

Foreign mission is a hugely important part of the church's work. Christianity is not a 'Western' thing, but a global thing. It always was. It originated in the Middle East, and then Paul was appointed as the apostle to the Gentiles. (Again Gentiles are the non-Jews, or the nations – in other words, the whole of the rest of the world.) People sometimes assume that no one realised long ago that there were different religions in different parts of the world. We only discovered this with increased exploration from the fifteenth century onwards, and now those of us who are enlightened understand that people in different parts of the world can find their way to God by different means. This is nonsense. In Acts 17, for example, you find Paul preaching in Athens, a city characterised by the worship of countless 'gods'. What does he say?

> The times of ignorance God overlooked, but now he commands *all people everywhere* to repent, because he has fixed a day on which he will judge the world in righteousness by a man whom he has appointed; and of this he has given assurance to all by raising him from the dead (Acts 17:30-31).

Paul is saying that Jesus Christ is going to judge *all people everywhere*, and so all people everywhere need to get right with God through him. There are millions of people throughout the world who have never heard a clear presentation of the gospel of Christ. His church needs to put that right, and that means you and me.

As well as the nations around the world, we should also have a particular concern for our own nation. There are few nations which need the gospel more badly than my own, the UK. Mark Greene of the *London Institute for Contemporary Christianity* likes to point out that, although Christians in our nation can feel like a little minority huddled in a corner, we're not. We are a minority, but we have a presence in homes, offices, schools, leisure spaces and communities throughout the land. As he puts it, 'We have the people. And we have them in place.'[2] The question is whether the people, in the places where God has put them, are willing to be used by him in the spread of the gospel.

2. The neighbours

That brings us from the nations to the neighbours. It's possible that you might be called to overseas missionary work, but most readers of this book will have a mission field much closer to home. Of the millions in the world who have never heard a clear presentation of the gospel of Christ, we rub shoulders with some of them every day. It might be your neighbours, your colleagues, or even your own family. Some have heard and rejected the gospel, but many have never heard it. Perhaps God has placed us where we are so that, in and through us, they might finally hear the gospel's message. If we don't tell them, who will?

We need to think about the people God has placed in our lives. For many, our children are one of the primary mission fields in our lives, or perhaps our grandchildren. Then there are others: the school gate, the office canteen, the staffroom, the golf club. In these contexts, we need to remember the centrality of the gospel and the urgency of its proclamation. That doesn't mean we become

[2] Mark Greene, *Imagine: How We Can Reach the UK* (Milton Keynes: Authentic, 2004), p. 44.

obnoxious bores who never let up. We need wisdom and grace. But neither should we sit idly by while people head towards an eternal destiny that is uncertain or worse. If you spend a lot of time at the golf club, you need to remember that it's no consolation to anyone to head off to hell with an impressive handicap.

The how: showing and sharing

Finally, what about the *how*? Again, we live in an age which is resource-rich and there are many books and other resources to help you to share your faith.[3] In the end, though, the two essential ingredients in effective personal evangelism are showing and sharing. There needs to be a showing of the gospel in the way that we live, and a sharing of the gospel by the words that we speak. Only by this will people come to understand what the Christian message is, and have the opportunity to respond to it.

Both elements are necessary. If we show God's love to others, genuinely building relationships, caring for others and living a godly life, and yet we never say that we're Christians or seek to share our faith with them, then we're not really doing evangelism at all. If our churches are engaging in all sorts of mercy ministries and social justice projects, but never proclaim Christ and him crucified, how will people ever know the source of this life and love that we have?

On the other hand, there's a way to declare the truths of the gospel which has far more to do with self-righteousness than with compassion for the lost. If we resolutely proclaim the message of the Bible, but consistently fail to build relationships with unbelievers through which they can come to know, respect and trust us, why should they listen? If we share that God is a God of

[3] Let me recommend John Chapman, *Know and Tell the Gospel* (New Malden: Good Book Company, 1998); John Dickson, *Promoting the Gospel* (Sydney: Blue Bottle Books, 2005); and Mark Dever, *The Gospel and Personal Evangelism* (Wheaton: Crossway, 2007).

compassion, but fail to show that through mercy ministries, why should anyone believe that the gospel changes hearts and lives?

This is one of the key things to grasp when it comes to personal evangelism. You may well feel entirely inadequate to share the gospel with anyone. Most of us do. However, for the vast majority of Christians, evangelism doesn't come out of giftedness but by relationship. People will listen when they're hearing the message from people they respect, people who have demonstrated that they are trustworthy, who have refrained from gossip, who have gone the extra mile. They'll listen when they hear it from people who don't hide their faith away and then half-shamefully reveal it, but are open about their faith and make it clear that it's just a part of who they are. These things earn a hearing. They open doors.

The rapid growth of the early church in Acts happened because Christians were thrilled to the core by what they had discovered. They were amazed by grace, and excited by the gospel, and it was the most natural thing in the world for them to tell the people who were around them about it.

God is sovereign in salvation, and dramatic conversions do happen, but research suggests that the average period from first gospel contact to conversion is around four years. That represents a lot of patient relationship-building, a lot of prayer, a lot of care, and a lot of love. More than ever, in this age which is suspicious of truth claims, people need Christians in their lives who will both share and show the gospel.

Conclusion: a foretaste of the joy of glory

When we understand what's at stake, we come to realise that there is no more important calling in life than to share the gospel of Christ. There is nothing more loving that we can do for anyone, and there is nothing more thrilling than to see God at work as we do it. John G. Paton, the nineteenth-century missionary to the New Hebrides in the Pacific that we read about in the previous chapter, describes how he laboured for three years, and at the end of that time was able to baptise twelve converts and establish a church. That happened on 24 October 1869, and the new believers shared in the Lord's Supper together:

> For three years we had toiled and prayed and taught for this. At the moment when I put the bread and wine into those dark hands, once stained with the blood of cannibalism, but now stretched out to receive and partake the emblems and seals of the Redeemer's love, I had a foretaste of the joy of Glory that well-nigh broke my heart to pieces. I shall never taste a deeper bliss till I gaze on the glorified face of Jesus himself.[4]

[4] Paton, *Autobiography*, p. 376.

CHAPTER TWELVE

Following Jesus Every Day:
The Essentials of Work

*Slaves, obey your earthly masters with fear and trembling, with a
sincere heart, as you would Christ, ⁶ not by the way of eye-service,
as people-pleasers, but as servants of Christ, doing the will of God
from the heart, ⁷ rendering service with a good will as to the Lord
and not to man, ⁸ knowing that whatever good anyone does,
this he will receive back from the Lord, whether he is a slave or
free. ⁹ Masters, do the same to them, and stop your threatening,
knowing that he who is both their Master and yours is in heaven,
and that there is no partiality with him.* – Ephesians 6:5-9.

Introduction

Leonard Woolf, who was the husband of Virginia Woolf and a civil
servant and author, wrote in his autobiography:

> Looking back at the age of eighty-eight over the fifty-seven years
> of my political work in England, knowing what I aimed at and the
> results, meditating on the history of Britain and the world since
> 1914, I see clearly that I have achieved practically nothing. The
> world today and the history of the human anthill during the past
> fifty-seven years would be exactly the same as it is if I had played
> ping pong instead of sitting on committees and writing books
> and memoranda. I have therefore to make the rather ignominious
> confession to myself and anyone who reads these words that I

must have in a long life ground through between 150,000 and 200,000 hours of perfectly useless work.[1]

How appalling to think that you could come to the end of a lifetime's work and be left with nothing more than the gnawing sense that none of it had any real significance! Work is a huge part of our lives – and let me say that what I'll be discussing in this chapter applies whatever your 'work' might be. It might be in an office, shop or school. It might be studying, or caring for family, or home-building. It could even be what they tell me is the busiest working environment of all, namely retirement. I'll be setting out the principles as they apply to an employment situation, but they're relevant whatever your daily life might involve.

Many of us have a love-hate relationship with work. When work *works*, and we spend our days doing something that brings us a sense of enjoyment and accomplishment, it energises us and lifts our spirits. But when work doesn't work, and we're trapped in a daily grind that we find tedious, or frustrating or pointless, it saps our energy and leaves us tired and depressed.

Given how huge a part of life this is for most of us, it's important that we think clearly about what the Bible has to say about work, and how the gospel affects it. What difference does our faith make to our working lives? What does Christianity mean from nine to five? These questions may or may not have occurred to you, because it's often assumed that faith and work are simply two different compartments of life. There might be some jobs where God is relevant, but what if I'm an I.T. consultant, or a secretary, or a barista in Starbucks? Is God really interested in the job that I do?

Christians seem to have an irresistible urge to build work-related spiritual hierarchies. At the bottom of the pile are people we know are just out to serve themselves, like bankers and hedge fund managers. (I have no idea what a hedge fund is, but I'm pretty sure

[1] Quoted in Tom L. Eisenman, *Temptations Men Face* (Downers Grove: IVP, 1990), p. 41.

it has nothing to do with landscape gardening. Anyway, apologies to my banking and investment readership for that last comment.) Then, a step up, you have those in the caring professions, like nurses and teachers. As a former litigator I've been trying to convince my congregation for years that law is one of the caring professions, but no one seems to be going for it. The next step in the hierarchy takes you to ministers or pastors, followed by a top tier of missionaries and world-famous Christian speakers and evangelists. That's how it works, isn't it?

The purpose of this chapter is to convince you otherwise. I want to persuade you that there's no such thing as 'secular' work; that all work has spiritual significance, whether you're funding hedges or hedging funds; and that all Christians are called to be Christians wherever they are and whatever they're doing. As long as we fail to see this, and treat our working lives as something separate and different, where the gospel has no impact, both our working lives and our Christian discipleship will be hugely impoverished.

Slaving away

We're going to be working from Ephesians 6:5-9, so it would be helpful for you to read that passage. If you do, unless you're already getting used to the Bible and have stopped asking the kinds of questions that are good to ask, an objection should arise in your mind. Why is Paul talking about slaves, and why is he telling them to obey their masters? Does the Bible condone slavery? That is a common claim, but it's a shallow and false one. The Bible undermines slavery at every turn, and the reason slavery was outlawed throughout the developed world is because Bible-believing Christians like William Wilberforce took on slavery and defeated it against all the odds. They did so, not despite their commitment to the Bible, but because of it.[2]

---

[2] For a more detailed treatment of Paul's views of slavery, and his underlying message of freedom see Scot McKnight, *The Letter to Philemon* (Grand Rapids: Eerdmans, 2017).

So if the Bible doesn't condone slavery, what is Paul doing in Ephesians 6? The answer is simple: he's writing to a church that is full of slaves. There are estimated to have been sixty million of them in the Roman Empire, including over half the population of Rome itself. There they all are, sitting in the congregation. Paul knows that, and so he addresses them. Otherwise you have to imagine an elder standing up at the start of the service and saying: 'This is a very special day. We've received a letter from Paul, the apostle. So we're going to read it together now; it's a wonderful explanation of the gospel and then he not only explains the gospel but he applies it to us, telling us how the gospel transforms every aspect of our lives… unless you're a slave. If you're a slave, Paul has nothing to say to you about how to live as a Christian where you are, and there will be a separate socialist revolution seminar after the service.'

The gospel is for all people, so it's addressed to all people. Besides, a first-century Graeco-Roman slave probably looked much more like a modern employee than you imagine. Slaves held all sorts of working positions throughout society.[3] That means that the principles Paul sets out are highly relevant and valuable to us as we consider how we're called to live out our working lives as followers of Christ. I want to make five statements which help us to form a biblical perspective on work.

The gospel respects work: it's not meaningless

First, the gospel respects work and affirms that it is not meaningless. Whatever it might feel like sometimes, work is not a terrible mistake or a necessary evil. It takes its place as part of the good creation that God made. In the opening chapters of Genesis we read that God created a perfect world. He then created a man, and this is what he did with him: 'The LORD God took the man and put him in the garden of Eden to work it and keep it' (Genesis 2:15). Here we have

[3] For a helpful perspective on this issue see Timothy Keller, *Every Good Endeavour* (London: Hodder & Stoughton), 2012, pp.280-283 (note 201).

the creation of work, and the drafting of the first job description: work the garden and keep it. Work doesn't begin after the Fall, when sin has entered the world and everything has gone wrong, but is there from the beginning as something good. God himself sets the pattern, working for six days and resting for one, and then he sets Adam working. That work was a gift to humanity, for our blessing and our joy, and part of the God-like status which is our unique privilege. That explains why work has the potential to be so fulfilling and rewarding, and why we want it to be like that. This is what we were made for.

So the problem is not work. The problem is what work *becomes* in a fallen and broken world. After Adam and Eve sin against God, a curse is placed on the serpent, and a curse is placed on humanity, but a curse is also placed on the world itself. God says to Adam:

> Because you have listened to the voice of your wife and have eaten of the tree of which I commanded you, 'You shall not eat of it', cursed is the ground because of you; in pain you shall eat of it all the days of your life; thorns and thistles it shall bring forth for you; and you shall eat the plants of the field. By the sweat of your face you shall eat bread, till you return to the ground… (Genesis 3:17-19).

Sin spoils us, it spoils our relationships and it spoils our environment. For all these reasons, it spoils our work. That is why the same work which can be so enriching and fulfilling, can also be so frustrating and wearisome. Instead of being a joyful expression of creative exuberance, reflecting the creativity of God himself, work starts to feel like painful toil. There are 'thorns and thistles' in every office, staff room and shop floor, making work wearisome. Work becomes shaped largely by self-interest, to the point that in almost every workplace there is almost constant conflict of one kind or another. If you doubt that, find any office, stand by the water cooler for five minutes, and listen: '… did you hear what he said… what a nerve that woman has… well I just said, that's not in my job description…'. Work is spoiled. Human sinfulness uses the working environment to serve self, and the cost is high. We lose honesty and integrity, and the determination to do a good job for a client or customer. We lose diligence and efficiency, and the sense of pride in a job well done. We lose harmony, teamwork and healthy working relationships. The presence of sin means that work breaks down at many levels.

The result is a strange mixture of great fulfilment and great frustration. There are still traces of the goodness of work's original design, but it has been badly spoiled and no longer perfectly fulfils the purposes which God intended for it.

Enter the gospel. The gospel is good news for work, and good news for workers. To begin with, it reminds and reassures us that work is a God-designed, God-created thing. But the gospel impacts our work at much deeper levels too. Ephesians 5–6 describes a wonderful two-way process in which the gospel transforms all of our relationships, and then all of our relationships come to be so much characterised by grace that they effectively display the gospel for the world to see. Paul has been speaking about how that works in marriage, and in the relationship between children and parents, and now between workers and employers. So that's where we are going: we want to see how disciples of Jesus can put the gospel on display by the way that we work, whether as an employer or employee.

The gospel relativizes work: it's not ultimate

Once work is fallen and infected by sin, there are two major dangers. The first is that work takes a place in our lives which it was never designed to have. Work becomes everything. It's like gangrene, spreading out of control and consuming everything it meets. Everything else has to give way before it, and work starts to take over our lives. It justifies our existence and creates our identity: I am what I do. That creates a horrible hierarchy in our society of those whose jobs are considered significant and valuable, and others who feel ashamed to admit at dinner parties what they do for a living. It also drives people to become workaholics. Most of us have seen at close hand the way that work can become the first priority in someone's life, often with devastating effects on their families and friendships. This is a kind of idolatry: we make work into our god, and we bow before it. It's the one non-negotiable, and everything else in life must fit around it.

The gospel relativizes work by reminding us that it is not ultimate. It's a good thing, and an important part of life, but it's not what we live for. Let me say clearly: if you're living for work, it will destroy you. It's a good servant, but it's a cruel god.

The way that the gospel counters this is by out-performing, and thereby destroying, all the motives that would make us idolise work. If we're tempted to let work take over because of our desire for material possessions or a certain lifestyle, the gospel reveals these as the transient things they really are. It replaces our desire for them with a desire for Christ and for the things of eternity. If we're tempted to let work take over because our self-esteem is bound up with our success at work, the gospel frees us from that slavery by showing us how utterly precious we are to the God who gave his Son for us. If we're tempted to let work take over for the sake of acceptance by colleagues and respect from superiors, the gospel shows how we are completely accepted in Christ and given a place of highest honour in him. If we're tempted to work too hard because of a desire for significance and for permanence, the gospel tells us that we will outlive the universe. As C. S. Lewis once put it, we will live to remember the galaxies as an old tale.[4]

The gospel therefore out-performs every motivation to give work a place that it shouldn't have. Above all, it places Christ before us in all his glory. When we have him steadily before our eyes, we will not be in danger of thinking that work is the meaning of life.

---

[4] C. S. Lewis, 'Membership' in *Essay Collection & Other Short Pieces* (London: Harper Collins, 2000), p. 339.

The gospel redeems work: it's not futile

If the first great danger about work in a fallen world is to believe that work is everything, the second is to believe that work is nothing. It has no real value in itself, and certainly no Christian significance. It's just a necessary evil, which we resent. The aim of work is to make as much money as possible, in as short a time as possible, by doing as little as possible, so that we can then go off and (insert preferred leisure pursuit here) as much as possible. Work in itself has no inherent significance unless we happen to achieve world peace or find a cure for cancer. We're back to Leonard Woolf: it's all just a waste of time and we'd be as well playing ping-pong.

There is a strange and amazing phenomenon in the natural world called the ant mill. Army ants are blind, and each one follows a chemical trail left by the ant in front of them. (Don't ask me how the first one knows where it's going.) Every now and then, one ant will go off course, and just keep walking. Other ants follow its scent, away from the main group, and eventually the first one wanders around until it finds its own pheromone trail. Round it goes, with other ants faithfully following on behind, until the ant trail forms a continuously rotating circle, or ant mill. These can be quite small, or a few metres across, but in 1921 a naturalist discovered one with a circumference of 1,200 feet. It took each ant two and a half hours to walk round to its starting-point.[5] Once the mill is formed, the ants march on in a completely pointless circle until, one by one, they die of exhaustion.

Is that what our work is like? Are we all just walking around in a big circle of going to work, buying food, watching TV, going to bed, getting up, going to work, buying food, watching TV, going to bed…until eventually one day we die?

The gospel frees us from that kind of despair and meaninglessness. The gospel redeems work, and assures us that it's not futile.

---

[5] William Beebe, *Edge of the Jungle* (New York: Henry Holt & Co., 1921), pp. 291-294.

It shows us that this world matters, and glorifying God in this world matters. As a race, we have been privileged with the stewardship of this planet, under God. The very first command in the Bible is: 'Be fruitful and multiply and fill the earth and subdue it and have dominion …' (Genesis 1:28). This is sometimes referred to as the 'cultural mandate', which is the idea that forming cultures and contributing to them productively through work is God's intention for us. It remains part of his purpose for the world, and therefore is part of what serving him involves. In taking part in that process for his glory, we are doing something meaningful which pleases him. New York pastor Tim Keller explains how our work involves taking the raw material of God's creation and rearranging it in such a way that it helps the world in general, and people in particular, to thrive and flourish.

> This pattern is found in all kinds of work. Farming takes the physical material of soil and seed, and produces food. Music takes the physics of sound and rearranges it into something beautiful and thrilling that brings meaning to life. When we take fabric and make a piece of clothing, when we push a broom and clean up a room, when we use technology to harness the forces of electricity, when we take an unformed naïve human mind and teach it a subject, when we take simple materials and turn them into a poignant work of art – we are continuing God's work of forming, filling and subduing. Whenever we bring order out of chaos, whenever we draw out creative potential, whenever we elaborate and 'unfold' creation beyond where it was when we found it, we are following God's pattern of creative cultural development. In fact, our word 'culture' comes from this idea of cultivation. Just as he subdued the earth in his work of creation, so he calls us now to labor as his representatives in a continuation and extension of that work of subduing.[6]

All of our work contributes in some way to the culture in which we live. That means you can forget everything that the world has

[6] Timothy Keller, *Every Good Endeavour*, p. 59.

told you about what work is important and what isn't, who has status and who doesn't, and which workers can make a difference and which can't. To see our work as a part of God's purpose for his world gives great honour and dignity to whatever we do from nine to five.

The gospel reorients work: it's not self-serving

Next, the gospel reorients work, so that we come to see that it's not self-serving. In a fallen world, work is all too easily focused on self-interest and self-promotion. Jesus would say to us: *it shall not be so among you.* Whether employer or employee, the Christian's whole view of life has been changed. We follow the one who came, not to be served but to serve, and when his Spirit controls us we become servants of others. The Christian life is the life of a servant, and if that is lived out consistently in a workplace, it will stand out a mile. It will bring something of the fragrance of heaven itself into the shop, or the office, or the staff room. Returning to Ephesians 6, here the Christian slave (or employee) is told to obey sincerely (verse 5) and render service with a good will (verse 7). In other words, Christian employees should be good employees. That means more than not stealing from the supplies cupboard or cheating on your expenses, or sleeping with your colleagues. It means that Christian workers should be people who understand what it is to serve, and who do so gladly. Christian workers should be the ones their team leaders would most hate to lose.

Paul then addresses masters, and what he says is simply stunning. Having told slaves to obey their earthly masters, rendering service with a good will, he now says, 'Masters, do the same to them...' (verse 9). There's the answer to our earlier question: if the Bible condones slavery, it's a form of slavery in which masters are called to obey their slaves! They are to use their authority to serve those who work for them, and that's revolutionary in any century, let alone the first! The reason for this radical command is given in verse 9: the Christian master is a follower of *the* Master, and should therefore pattern his leadership after that of Christ. Jesus, although he was in very nature God, did not consider equality with God something to be grasped, but made himself nothing, taking on the very nature of… a slave (Philippians 2:6-7).

In this way, Christians in the workplace are almost dramatising the gospel, as leaders and servants together reflect the character of their servant leader. Employers demonstrate what it is to lead with sacrificial love, and employees demonstrate what it is to serve with glad submission. This is why Christians should be, and how they can be, distinctive in the workplace. The gospel reorients work.

The gospel refocuses work: it's for the glory of God

A final key insight from Ephesians 6 which underpins all of our thinking about work is that the gospel refocuses work, showing us that it's for the glory of God. Repeatedly in these verses Paul returns to the fundamental insight that, as Christians, we are all working first and foremost for Christ. He drives this home repeatedly. At verse 5 he tells slaves to obey their earthly masters *as they would Christ*. At verse 6 he urges them to obey *as servants of Christ*. At verse 7 he tells them to serve *as to the Lord* and not man. In the equivalent passage in Colossians, he says: 'Whatever you do, work heartily, as for the Lord and not for men, knowing that from the Lord you will receive the inheritance as your reward. You are serving the Lord Christ' (Colossians 3:23-24).

To say that we are working for Christ in everything is not a pious fiction, but reality. He is sovereign over every moment of every day, over every breath you take and everything you do. That, ultimately, is why all work has great dignity and supreme significance – because we are, every one of us, honoured servants of the King. What we do, we do for his glory. If a first-century slave can glorify God in his work, then who of us can say that we can't?

So if you go into work tomorrow, all fired up to fulfil the cultural mandate and reflect the gospel of grace in your relationships, and your boss is a tyrant... or unreasonable... or just stupid; as a frustrated employee at the end of your tether, but a Christian employee, what do you do? How do you obey in a God-honouring, grace-filled manner? There is only one way: by remembering that you're working for Christ. This is the only way that you will ever be able to do it. You look over your boss's shoulder, and you see standing there the one you're really serving. Would you obey Christ? Then obey your boss. Would you serve Christ? Then serve your boss. That's how to live out the gospel. It's when we have Christ in our mind's eye that we're enabled to serve respectfully and sincerely, and not only when we'll be recognised and rewarded, but when no one is looking and perhaps when no one will even notice what we've done. Christ sees all, and Paul assures us that 'whatever good anyone does, this he will receive back from the Lord' (verse 8). It's good to know, in this world where some aspects of work can feel so futile, that nothing you do for Christ's sake will ever be in vain.

Christian discipleship is about following Jesus every day, everywhere, in everything. That means that our work will always be a central part of our Christian life, and never separated off as if God doesn't reign there. Instead, we refocus work, away from self-service and towards the glory of God. In the midst of a fallen world where work has so often become an arena for the outworking of human selfishness, if Christians will live and work in these ways faithfully and consistently, their light will shine for the glory of their Father in heaven (Matthew 5:16).

Conclusion

Who would have thought that in the ordinary grind of nine to five, ordinary Christians performing ordinary tasks could display the character of God and of his gospel to the world? Writing to Titus, Paul beautifully describes what the outcome of such a life will be:

> Slaves are to be submissive to their own masters in everything; they are to be well-pleasing, not argumentative, not pilfering, but

showing all good faith, so that in everything they may adorn the doctrine of God our Saviour (Titus 2:9-10).

What a glorious calling. As you teach, do the filing, change nappies, make phone calls, care for grandchildren, paint, clean up vomit, draft a contract, meet with a client, feed an elderly relative – whatever you're doing this week – hand that task over to Christ, performing it in his service. He will see it. He will reward it. And when you perform it in willing obedience to him, you adorn the gospel. You commend it, you show forth its beauty, and you bring glory to God.

CHAPTER THIRTEEN

Following Jesus with All We Have: The Essentials of Stewardship

Now there is great gain in godliness with contentment, ⁷ for we brought nothing into the world, and we cannot take anything out of the world. ⁸ But if we have food and clothing, with these we will be content. ⁹ But those who desire to be rich fall into temptation, into a snare, into many senseless and harmful desires that plunge people into ruin and destruction. ¹⁰ For the love of money is a root of all kinds of evils. It is through this craving that some have wandered away from the faith and pierced themselves with many pangs.

¹¹ But as for you, O man of God, flee these things. Pursue righteousness, godliness, faith, love, steadfastness, gentleness. ¹² Fight the good fight of the faith. Take hold of the eternal life to which you were called and about which you made the good confession in the presence of many witnesses. ¹³ I charge you in the presence of God, who gives life to all things, and of Christ Jesus, who in his testimony before Pontius Pilate made the good confession, ¹⁴ to keep the commandment unstained and free from reproach until the appearing of our Lord Jesus Christ, ¹⁵ which he will display at the proper time – he who is the blessed and only Sovereign, the King of kings and Lord of lords, ¹⁶ who alone has immortality, who dwells in unapproachable light, whom no one has ever seen or can see. To him be honour and eternal dominion. Amen. ¹⁷ As for the rich in this present age, charge them not to be haughty, nor to set their hopes on the uncertainty of riches, but on God, who richly provides us with everything to enjoy. ¹⁸ They are to do

> good, to be rich in good works, to be generous and ready to share, [19] thus storing up treasure for themselves as a good foundation for the future, so that they may take hold of that which is truly life.
>
> – 1 Timothy 6:6-19.

Introduction: you are rich

Across the world, almost two billion people live on less than £1 per day. Something that we put in a shopping trolley is life or death to billions of people. Equally startling is the fact that the richest fifth of the world's population possesses seventy five percent of the world's wealth; the next two fifths control another twenty percent; which means that the remaining five percent of the world's wealth is shared out amongst forty percent of the world's people.

My purpose in mentioning these statistics is very simple: I want you to recognise that *you are rich*. You probably picked up this book not thinking of yourself as rich, but I want you to acknowledge in your mind now that you are. Unless this book has reached corners of the world I haven't anticipated, you and I have a standard of living far above that of most human beings. Over time we all come to think of the way we live as normal, but it's not. You are rich.

I emphasise this because I want you to realise how much danger you're in. Listen to these words of Jesus: 'How difficult it will be for those who have wealth to enter the kingdom of God!' (Mark 10:23) When he said it, he was looking with sadness at a man we know as the rich young ruler: a man who had no electric lights, no central heating, no hygienic plumbing, no car, no flatscreen TV and no smartphone. 'How difficult it will be', said Jesus. How easy it is for the wealthy to miss everything that is most important.

Since we're so rich, the subject of stewardship – how we handle what we have – is a very important one for us. This may be why the Bible in general, and Jesus in particular, has so much to say about it. He speaks about it often, as do the writers of the New Testament. They recognise that fallen men and women tend to worship created things rather than the Creator. We tend to look to them rather than him for our happiness, our security and even sometimes our identity. So as you read through the Bible, expect the subject of money to come up a lot.

Stewardship relates to everything that God has given us, including possessions, time and gifts, but for the purposes of this chapter I'm going to focus on how we handle money. The aim is to get an overview of the Bible's teaching on these things, so that we're beginning to form a biblical mindset. We'll consider four passages from the Bible, two of which concern our attitude to having money, and two of which concern our attitude to giving it away.

Nothing in, nothing out: remembering what matters

Humour me for a moment as we perform a thought experiment. Imagine that you and several others have been locked in a room for twenty-four hours. Inside the room is a certain amount of money and goods. The rules are that you take nothing in with you, and after the twenty-four hours are up, you will all leave the room and take nothing out. The question is: what would you be willing to do in order to gain an increased share of the money and goods in the room for yourself? Would you give every waking moment to the accumulation of these possessions? Would you destroy your relationships with the others in the room, in order to get your hands on more stuff? Would you cheat others in order to accumulate more? Would you lie? Would you kill?

It's ridiculous, isn't it? Yet, in a life which they entered with nothing and will leave with nothing, people do all these things and more for the sake of money. Have a look at 1 Timothy 6:6-19. Paul begins that passage with a striking statement: 'Now there is great gain in godliness with contentment, for we brought nothing into the world, and we cannot take anything out of the world.'

This is our first lesson in stewardship: nothing in, nothing out. One day soon we will leave this earth, and we will leave everything behind. We need this perspective in order to keep our attitude to money in its rightful place, but two factors make it very difficult. First, our sinful, selfish hearts want to accumulate stuff. Secondly, the wrongful desires of those hearts are reinforced continually by the culture in which we live, which lies to us about money and possessions, and does so every hour of every day, and never stops. In the absence of 'godliness with contentment', our culture lives as if the enjoyment of the things of this world were the greatest good. If there is nothing greater to live for and nothing beyond the grave, the outcome is inevitable: eat, drink and be merry, for tomorrow we die. Or as someone has put it: 'Crave and spend, for the Kingdom of Stuff is here.'[1] Without a firm eternal perspective, possessions are inevitably given a significance greater than they should have, and the result is untold selfishness and misery.

In contrast to that, and remembering how we define 'the rich', look at how Paul calls on Christians to live:

> As for the rich in this present age, charge them not to be haughty, nor to set their hopes on the uncertainty of riches, but on God, who richly provides us with everything to enjoy. They are to do good, to be rich in good works, to be generous and ready to share, thus storing up treasure for themselves as a good foundation for the future, so that they may take hold of that which is truly life (1 Timothy 6:17-19).

Do you see how thoroughly counter-cultural this is? *The way to store up treasure for yourself is to be quick to give it away.* Nothing could be more different from the consumerist mentality of our culture, but we're being reminded that godliness is of greater value than financial gain. As we consider what to do with the capital of our lives, we need to invest in eternity more than in now.

None of this means that we don't need money and possessions. We all live in this world and we all have bills to pay, but God has

---

[1] Mark Buchanan, 'Trapped in the Cult of the Next Thing', *Christianity Today*, 6 September 1999, pp. 63-72.

asked us to live for him. So while we will all have money and things, stewardship is about how we handle what we have. Christian stewardship demands a radical realignment of our relationship with money and possessions. Given the rampant materialism and consumerism of the modern West, if we take that seriously, we should stick out like sore thumbs. If our faith is genuinely impacting our lives, we should be making decisions all the time which make no sense at all to people who don't share that faith. People around us should be simultaneously amazed, perplexed and curious because our attitude to money is so different from theirs.

Here are two basic things which should characterise the Christian's approach to money. First, it should simply be far less important to us than it is to others. We have something far more precious and lasting that puts the things of this world into perspective. We do *not* believe the bumper sticker that declares that 'he who dies with the most toys wins'. Therefore, as Paul puts it, we 'do not set [our] hopes on the uncertainty of riches, but on God' (1 Timothy 6:17). That relativizes the significance of money, so that its grip on our hearts is loosened.

Secondly, and more profoundly still, we recognise that everything we have belongs to God. We are stewards, entrusted with the temporary care of something which belongs to someone else. Your money may feel like your own, but the Bible tells us that 'Every good gift… is from above, coming down from the Father…' (James 1:17). This means that the real breakthrough in Christian stewardship comes, not when we decide to treat a reasonable proportion of what we have *as if it belonged to God*, but when we come to see that everything we have *does belong to God*. Only then will we be released from the tyranny of materialism, and freed to give generously and joyfully for the good of the gospel and the glory of God.

Christian stewardship entails a radical reassessment of our relationship with money and possessions.

The secret of contentment: remembering whose we are

Let me now draw your attention to a second passage that helps us to summarise the impact of that reassessment. If there is one word which more than any other encapsulates the Bible's teaching on how we should view our finances and our circumstances, it's the word 'contentment'. It crops up in various places in the Bible, at crucial points in discussions of stewardship and generosity. In the New Testament period, the church in Philippi made a contribution to support the apostle Paul's missionary work, and this is how he responded to them:

> I rejoiced in the Lord greatly that now at length you have revived your concern for me. You were indeed concerned for me, but you had no opportunity. Not that I am speaking of being in need, for I have learned in whatever situation I am to be content. I know how to be brought low, and I know how to abound. In any and every circumstance, I have learned the secret of facing plenty and hunger, abundance and need. I can do all things through him who strengthens me (Philippians 4:10-13).

'I have learned the secret,' he says. 'I can do all things *through him who strengthens me.*' The secret of contentment is not to remember what we have, but to remember whose we are. Paul can accept his circumstances with confidence and assurance, whatever they might be, because he is secure in God himself. Nothing else in the world can replace the security that comes with the knowledge that you are held in the hands of the living God. Not even the best of human relationships can do that, never mind money. The same point comes across particularly clearly at Hebrews 13:5-6. 'Keep your life free from love of money, and be content with what you have, for he has said, "I will never leave you or forsake you." So we can confidently say, "The Lord is my helper; I will not fear."'

This sense of rock-solid confidence and stability is absolutely independent of financial security, and enables us to be content with what we have, rather than always grasping after more. That should protect us from the consumerist mentality of our culture. For example, Christians should watch and listen to adverts in a different way from non-Christians. In fact, I would go so far as to say that a Christian who knows the kind of contentment that the Bible holds out to us should be largely immune from advertising. Back in the 1980s, a New York professor called Neil Postman wrote a fascinating book called *Amusing Ourselves to Death*, about the impact that television has on culture. He wasn't a Christian, but there is much in his book that resonates with biblical thought. This is what he says about TV advertising:

> … the television commercial is not at all about the character of products to be consumed. It is about the character of the consumers of products. Images of movie stars and famous athletes, of serene lakes and macho fishing trips, of elegant dinners and romantic interludes, of happy families packing their station wagons for a picnic in the country – these tell nothing about the products being sold. But they tell everything about the fears, fancies and dreams of those who might buy them. What the advertiser needs to know is not what is right about the product but what is wrong about the buyer.[2]

In other words, advertising feeds on our insecurities. It tells us that we're missing out on the life we really deserve, or the product that will make us happy or secure. But Christians are instead invited and commanded to find their joy and their security in God himself. When we watch adverts, we shouldn't respond with 'I want one of those,' but with 'I know what you're doing. You're not fooling me. I know that you're trying to stir up dissatisfaction and discontentment with my life, and I'm not falling for it.'

So Christ's people, instead of running around chasing after the latest thing, are freed to live a simple life. I would want to commend that to you. Don't overload yourself with financial commitments. Don't strain towards the highest possible standard of living that you

---

[2] Neil Postman, *Amusing Ourselves to Death* (London: Methuen, 1987), p. 131.

could afford (or preferably a bit higher yet). Don't feel obligated to buy the most expensive house your salary permits, or the nicest car, or the newest clothes. Don't be a slave to the lifestyle the people around you have chosen. Instead, again contemplate what Paul wrote to Timothy:

> Now there is great gain in godliness with contentment, for we brought nothing into the world, and we cannot take anything out of the world. But if we have food and clothing, with these we will be content. But those who desire to be rich fall into temptation, into a snare, into many senseless and harmful desires that plunge people into ruin and destruction. For the love of money is a root of all kinds of evils. It is through this craving that some have wandered away from the faith (1 Timothy 6:6-10).

If ever there was a verse in the Bible that challenges our lifestyle to the core, it must be 1 Timothy 6:8 – 'But if we have food and clothing, with these we will be content.' Would *we*?

God's grace abounding: remembering what we have

In Paul's day the church didn't just give to support his missionary work, there was also a significant collection taken up for poor Christians in Jerusalem. Paul wrote to the Corinthian church to encourage their generous giving:

> The point is this: whoever sows sparingly will also reap sparingly, and whoever sows bountifully will also reap bountifully. Each one must give as he has decided in his heart, not reluctantly or under compulsion, for God loves a cheerful giver. And God is able to make all grace abound to you, so that having all sufficiency in all things at all times, you may abound in every good work (2 Corinthians 9:6-8)

The Greek word for 'cheerfulness', by the way, is where we get our word 'hilarious'. I love that: God loves a hilarious giver! The point of the section is very simple: our stewardship comes out of the recognition of God's enormous generosity towards us. We recognise

God's grace abounding in our own lives, and this motivates Christian giving which is glad, willing and joyful. It happens when we stop to think about what God has done for us, and come to realise the generosity of his provision for all of our needs.

Here's a challenge: do you spend more time thinking about what you don't have and planning to get it, or thinking about what you do have and thanking God for it? We need to discipline ourselves to remember – because it does not come naturally – that every good thing in our lives is only ours because God chose to give it to us. He richly provides us with everything to enjoy, making day-by-day provision of all that we need. And as we consider what God asks of us in terms of our stewardship, we have his promise that he will continue to provide for our needs. Notice how anxious Paul is to emphasise the sufficiency and generosity of God's provision: 'God is able to make all grace abound to you, so that having *all* sufficiency in *all* things at *all* times, you may abound in *every* good work.' The Christian whose needs are taken care of is freed to give for the care of the poor and to help advance the gospel.

Can you see how this propels stewardship in a certain direction? It becomes increasingly clear that God asks his people, not just to 'put something in the offering plate', but to be deliberate and generous and joyful about our giving. It doesn't honour God and demonstrate how precious he is to me if I grudgingly put something in the plate because I suppose I should, or if I try to figure out the minimum I have to give, or if I spend my time wondering what everyone else is giving. When we come to recognise God's grace abounding to us, one of the results is glad and generous giving. When a heart is gripped by grace, its instinctive response is not to hold back, limiting what we might be willing to give, but rather to strain forward, longing to support God's work as much as we can. We stop asking, 'How much do I *have* to give?' and start asking, 'How much *could* I give? How can I express my gratitude for all that God has done for me?'

Joy overflowing in generosity: the heart of the matter

Let's turn to one final passage to see how this works. Paul uses a lovely expression in 2 Corinthians 8 to describe the way in which some of the churches had contributed to the offering for Jerusalem.

> We want you to know, brothers, about the grace of God that has been given among the churches of Macedonia, for in a severe test of affliction, their abundance of joy and their extreme poverty have overflowed in a wealth of generosity on their part. For they gave according to their means, as I can testify, and beyond their means, of their own accord, begging us earnestly for the favour of taking part in the relief of the saints... (2 Corinthians 8:1-4).

This is what Christian stewardship is all about: joy overflowing in generosity. In the gospel, we experience the grace of God shown to us. We see that he has lavished goodness and mercy upon us which we did not deserve, and this grace transforms us from the inside out.

The power of grace to liberate and to transform, as opposed to the deadening impact of legalism and earning our way into God's favour, is the main thread in the storyline of *Les Miserables*. The whole story is about the transformation of Jean Valjean's life by the experience of grace that was granted to him, so that instead of taking from others he becomes a giver. The power of grace is highlighted by the contrast with Inspector Javert, whose life is defined by law. In the 2012 movie version, Javert insists, 'I am the Law, and the Law is not mocked.' He cannot comprehend grace, and when he sees something of the renewed heart of Jean Valjean, and something of this grace is extended to him, he just can't deal with it:

> I am reaching, but I fall,
>   and the stars are black and cold,
> as I stare into the void
>   of a world that cannot hold.

He cannot comprehend 'the world of Jean Valjean' – this power of grace, this force that is so alien to everything he has ever lived for. He is undone by it.

This is tragic, because to the one who grasps and receives it, like Valjean, grace opens up a world of generosity we could never otherwise have known. That is why, as Paul appeals to the Corinthians to give generously for the poor in Jerusalem, he seeks to motivate them not by a sense of guilt or of duty, but by the gospel itself. 'For you know the grace of our Lord Jesus Christ, that though he was rich, yet for your sake he became poor, so that you by his poverty might become rich' (2 Corinthians 8:9).

The gospel of God's grace makes us rich, in every way that matters and in every way that lasts, and that should make us deeply generous people. The gospel helps us to see more clearly how everything we have belongs to God. It loosens our attachment to the things of this world, because they are so clearly unimportant in comparison with the things of eternity. It prompts a new motivation in us to give in order to support the proclamation of the gospel throughout a world that so desperately needs to hear about Christ. It gives us a new power to give, opening our hearts and hands in ways that would otherwise be impossible.

One important aspect of Christian stewardship is that believers are called to support Christian ministry. In the normal course, we should direct the bulk of our giving to the local church to which we belong. I say that unashamedly, since ministry happens in the local church. It can only happen with financial support, and only Christians are going to provide it. So the local church is the priority, but there may well be other Christian work which we want to support, including Christian agencies which work with the poor, in this country and throughout the world, to make the love of Christ known in deeds as well as in words.

In the Old Testament, God's people were commanded to bring one tenth of their income to God. This specific commandment is not directly binding on Christians today, because it forms part of the laws of ancient Israel which were for that time and place. It would seem strange to conclude, however, that we have reason to be *less* generous. While the New Testament does not set down specific numbers or percentages, it gives us principles to guide our minds and motives that shape our hearts. Christian giving should be committed, deliberate and regular. It should be proportionate to our income, but it should also be sacrificial. By that I mean our giving should be at a level which means that we need to *sacrifice* other things so our lustful hearts might naturally want. We don't do that because there's some merit in making ourselves suffer, but because we want to be clear that Christ is more precious to us than anything else. We're also commanded to make the gospel known throughout the world, and being amongst the twenty percent of the world that holds seventy-five percent of the wealth, surely we have a particular responsibility to do that. This is simply part of what it means to be a follower of Jesus Christ, and to live for the glory of his name.

CHAPTER FOURTEEN

Following Jesus When It Hurts:
The Essentials of Suffering

Blessed be the God and Father of our Lord Jesus Christ! According to his great mercy, he has caused us to be born again to a living hope through the resurrection of Jesus Christ from the dead, [4] to an inheritance that is imperishable, undefiled, and unfading, kept in heaven for you, [5] who by God's power are being guarded through faith for a salvation ready to be revealed in the last time. [6] In this you rejoice, though now for a little while, if necessary, you have been grieved by various trials, [7] so that the tested genuineness of your faith – more precious than gold that perishes though it is tested by fire – may be found to result in praise and glory and honour at the revelation of Jesus Christ. [8] Though you have not seen him, you love him. Though you do not now see him, you believe in him and rejoice with joy that is inexpressible and filled with glory, [9] obtaining the outcome of your faith, the salvation of your souls.

[10] Concerning this salvation, the prophets who prophesied about the grace that was to be yours searched and enquired carefully, [11] enquiring what person or time the Spirit of Christ in them was indicating when he predicted the sufferings of Christ and the subsequent glories. [12] It was revealed to them that they were serving not themselves but you, in the things that have now been announced to you through those who preached the good news to you by the Holy Spirit sent from heaven, things into which angels long to look. – 1 Peter 1:3-12.

Introduction: the intolerable compliment

C. S. Lewis put it like this:

> We are, not metaphorically but in very truth, a Divine work of
> art, something that God is making, and therefore something
> with which he will not be satisfied until it has a certain character.
> Here again we come up against what I have called the 'intolerable
> compliment'. Over a sketch made idly to amuse a child, an artist
> may not take much trouble: he may be content to let it go even
> though it is not exactly as he meant it to be. But over the great
> picture of his life – the work which he loves, though in a different
> fashion, as intensely as a man loves a woman or a mother or
> a child – he will take endless trouble – and would, doubtless,
> thereby give endless trouble to the picture if it were sentient. One
> can imagine a sentient picture, after being rubbed and scraped
> and recommenced for the tenth time, wishing that it were only
> a thumbnail sketch whose making was over in a minute. In the
> same way, it is natural for us to wish that God had designed for us
> a less glorious and less arduous destiny; but then we are wishing
> not for more love but for less.[1]

The question of suffering has puzzled the brightest philosophical
minds for thousands of years. Why are our lives so marred by pain?
Why do some people have to endure so much, while others seem
to walk through life relatively unscathed? And how can these things
be consistent with the existence of a perfectly good and completely
powerful God? Why would he not eliminate suffering, or at least
make sure that all the suffering in the world was portioned out in
seven or eight billion equal slices?

The problem is arguably even more acute for Christians. Not
only does this loving and saving God allow them to continue to
undergo suffering, but sometimes their suffering is actually *inten-
sified* because of their commitment to him. That was the experience
of many people in the early church, and it remains the experience
of Christians in many parts of the world today. Even for those of

[1] C. S. Lewis, *The Problem of Pain* (London: Harper Collins, 1998), p. 28.

us who don't face violent persecution, the marginalisation and mockery of Christians can be a painful experience. So how do we keep on following Jesus when it hurts?

There's a strong argument that the existence of evil in the world is a reason to believe, rather than disbelieve in God. The concept of evil can only make any sense if there is such a thing as moral reality, and moral reality can only exist against an absolute standard by which it is measured. However, the purpose of this chapter is not to provide a philosophical answer to the problem of pain. If you want a Christian perspective on that, turn to Appendix 2. There we find that, far from being inconsistent with the existence of suffering, only a Christian worldview explains where suffering came from, why it feels so wrong, and how it can ultimately be overcome.

For now, we're going to attempt a more practical question: given that suffering is a reality in our lives, and not least in our Christian lives, what are we going to do with it? What use are we going to make of it? If we believe (as we should) that God is in charge of all things, that means he is sovereign over our suffering too. If his wisdom governs all things, it governs our suffering too. If he has a purpose in all things, he has a purpose in our suffering too. It may come to us sometimes as an intolerable compliment, but how does it change our experience of suffering when we understand that it falls within the sovereignty and loving purpose of our God? And if we're seeking to respond in a godly way to all that life brings, what does a godly response to suffering look like? Once you notice it, it's amazing how much of the Bible is given over to the task of encouraging God's people to persevere in hard times. In the Bible, in the history of the church and in the lives of individual Christians, we so often see God using the suffering of his people to accomplish his purposes. So how do we make good use of our suffering?

A caution: right and wrong questions

First let me sound a note of caution, because this is an area where Christians often misunderstand biblical teaching. There are parts of the Bible where God says that obedience to him will result in blessing, and disobedience will result in curse. As a general principle this is true and important: God has designed the world in a certain way, and we flourish where we live in line with his purposes. The problem arises where this general principle comes to be applied in a wooden and mechanical way: if something bad happens to you, it must be because you've done something wrong. If you know the book of Job at all, you'll know that the reason Job's friends were so useless, and the reason 'Job's comforters' is a proverbial expression for people who aren't comforters at all, is because this wooden and mechanical understanding was all they had to offer: if Job was suffering, he must have sinned. In fact, since Job was suffering a great deal… well, you can follow the logic.

We see the same logic on display during Jesus' day. In John 9:2, confronted with a man who was born blind, Jesus' disciples immediately asked him, 'Rabbi, who sinned, this man or his parents, that he was born blind?' They assumed that this suffering must have been caused by someone's sin.

We know that actions have consequences, and sometimes these can be severe. Old sins cast long shadows, and there are times when we suffer because of our own sinful folly. But it's one thing to say that your sin of adultery resulted in the devastating loss of your family; it's quite another to say that it led to your having cancer. The Bible teaches that suffering is caused by sin in a general sense. God's world was created perfect and free of pain, and suffering entered as an unwelcome intruder because of the Fall of Adam and Eve. But nowhere are we taught that the suffering of individuals is directly caused by their own sin. One of the main purposes of the book of Job is to teach us that such a view is muddle-headed. It takes a general principle of life, treats it an inflexible law of God, and in the process turns it into something that is misleading and spiritually crippling. That means that we should neither 'play God' by making such a judgment about others, nor assume that such a hard-and-fast rule applies to our own lives. There are religions in the world, such as certain forms of Hinduism and New Age religion, which teach a principle of *karma* in such a way that god (or fate) gives you what you deserve. In reality, applying that assumption to others is inevitably judgmental and applying it to yourself is inevitably torture. Throughout history, people have suffered all kinds of guilt by assuming that their suffering, or that of loved ones is God's punishment for something that they have done. We don't know if the parents of the man who was born blind made that assumption, but imagine if they did. Every day for decades, they would have blamed themselves for the blindness which they had inflicted on their son. What did Jesus say? 'It was not that this man sinned, or his parents…' (John 9:3). Jesus cut right across the received wisdom of his day to show that God's word had been misunderstood and misapplied, and in the process he liberated them from their misapprehension. He made clear that his disciples were simply asking the wrong question.

Professor Sir Norman Anderson was an English lawyer and evangelist who spent his life in the service of God. Along the way his son Hugh, after a brilliant university career, died of cancer at the age of twenty-one. Four years later, his two remaining children also died. By the early 1990s his wife, to whom he had been married for sixty years, was suffering from dementia to the extent that she could no longer recognise him. He was, in other words, a modern-day Job. In his mid-eighties, at one of his final public speaking engagements, he was asked: 'When you look back over your life and reflect on the fact that you have lost all your three children, and how your wife of sixty years no longer recognizes you, do you ever ask the question, "Why me?"' This was his response:

> No, I've never asked that question, 'Why me?' but I have asked the question, 'Why not me?' I am not promised as a Christian that I will escape the problems encountered by others; we all live in a fallen world…. I am however, promised that in the midst of difficulties, God through Christ will be present with me, and will give his grace to help me cope with the difficulties and bear witness to him.

Anderson went on to explain that the really vital question to ask God is not why he has allowed suffering in our lives, but what he wants to teach us through it.[2]

That, surely, is the key. When tragedy strikes we all ask why, but there are two ways to ask why. There's a backward-looking why: what caused this? ('Who sinned, this man or his parents…?') That question is almost always pointless and destructive. But there's also a forward-looking why: what might God be doing in my life through this? What can I learn from this? How can I grow through this? How can I use my suffering well?

So in that spirit, we're going to spend the rest of this chapter asking what our suffering can accomplish for us, what it can accomplish for others, and what it can accomplish for God.

What our suffering does for us: sanctification

When Peter wrote his first letter, it's likely that he was in Rome and that his readers (scattered throughout much of what we would call Turkey) were facing increasing social marginalisation for their new faith. They were probably not yet facing outright persecution, but the infamous Nero was emperor and the signs were not good. It wouldn't be long before he would blame Christians for the great fire of Rome and use it as an excuse to inflict horrible violence on them. So Peter's letter was no abstract thesis. He was addressing real people who were facing real suffering, but he went to great lengths to place that suffering in its rightful perspective and reassure them that there

[2] Howard Guinness, *Sacrifice* (1936), in Lindsay Brown, *Shining Like Stars: the Power of the Gospel in the World's Universities* (Nottingham: IVP, 2006), pp. 160-161.

was divine purpose in it:

> … now for a little while, if necessary, you have been grieved by various trials, so that the tested genuineness of your faith – more precious than gold that perishes though it is tested by fire – may be found to result in praise and glory and honor at the revelation of Jesus Christ (1 Peter 1:6-7).

Suffering serves the purpose of demonstrating that our faith is genuine. The refining process removes impurities from gold. All the worthless dross is removed so that what is left is pure, precious and lasting. Peter is hinting that we need suffering to refine our faith, because it has impurities. Yes, we trust in Christ – but not completely, and not always, and not exclusively. In our heart of hearts, we believe that our ultimate good depends on Jesus… and something else. We must have health, financial security, respect or whatever else is central to our identity. So sometimes these things are taken from us in order to purify and strengthen our faith, driving us to Jesus as our *only* source of security, peace and hope.

Faith that has been refined and proved to be genuine is a faith that fixes itself *completely* on Christ. Peter goes on to say at verse 8, 'Though you have not seen him, you love him. Though you do not now see him, you believe in him….' That is the very definition of faith: being sure of what we hope for and certain of what we do not see (Hebrews 11:1). Trials help us to rely completely for our ultimate good on the Saviour whom we cannot yet see. They teach us one of life's most profound lessons: that the only way to make sure that your greatest treasure is never taken away from you is to make sure that Christ is your greatest treasure. This is faith with the dross removed, pure, strong and precious.

The Bible frequently encourages us to consider the positive impact of negative experiences. Paul reminds us that 'suffering produces endurance, and endurance produces character, and character produces hope' (Romans 5:3-4). That could come across as trite, but not from the lips of Paul. This is how Jesus spoke of his purposes for Paul: '... he is a chosen instrument of mine to carry my name before the Gentiles and kings and the children of Israel. For I will show him how much he must suffer for the sake of my name' (Acts 9:15-16).

Peter tells suffering Christians that their suffering too is part of God's call upon their lives, and that it can be used to bring about good. Learning to trust amidst pain is part of Christian discipleship, and the only way you can learn to endure suffering is by suffering. It may seem surprising, but this is something that even Jesus himself had to learn.

> In the days of his flesh, Jesus offered up prayers and supplications, with loud cries and tears, to him who was able to save him from death.... Although he was a son, he learned obedience through what he suffered (Hebrews 5:7-8).

It's not that he was disobedient and learned to be obedient. It's that he learned what obedience to God looked like as it descended further and further into pain.

Suffering is one of the main ways in which God does deep soul-work within us. He takes us to places we would never have gone, and circumstances we would never have chosen; and in these places, and at these times, we learn things that we could never otherwise have known. We meet with God in ways we could never otherwise have met with him. In a unique way, God is there to be found at the end of your tether.

So suffering doesn't necessarily mean that you've offended God, and success doesn't necessarily mean that you've pleased him. In fact, the opposite may sometimes be true. The example of Jesus himself, as he went to the cross of Calvary, proves that it's possible to be exactly where God has placed you, and to be doing exactly what God has asked you to do, and yet to be in agony. This is the great clue, and the theme which Peter develops in 1 Peter 2:21-23.

> For to this you have been called, because Christ also suffered for you, leaving you an example, so that you might follow in

his steps. He committed no sin, neither was deceit found in his mouth. When he was reviled, he did not revile in return; when he suffered, he did not threaten, but continued entrusting himself to him who judges justly.

In other words, our suffering is to follow after the pattern of Christ. Paul describes how he longed to know 'the fellowship of his sufferings' (Philippians 3:10, KJV). We therefore look to the one who was known as the Man of Sorrows and the Suffering Servant, as both the model and the motive for our endurance of suffering. George Macdonald said: 'The Son of God suffered unto the death, not that men might not suffer, but that their sufferings might be like his.'[3]

Peter gives us a striking picture to drive the point home. Where he says that Christ left us an 'example', the Greek word he uses is *hypogrammos*, and it's a classroom word. Did you ever have to write out *The quick brown fox jumped over the lazy dog*? It's a sentence containing all the letters of the English alphabet, which children once had to write out repeatedly to 'learn their letters'. Fascinatingly, Clement of Alexandria, writing around AD 200, gave examples of equivalent Greek sentences which were used to do exactly the same thing for children then.[4] That's a *hypogrammos*. It's a sheet of paper with letters or sentences set out so that children could learn to write by tracing over what was already there. Jesus suffered, says Peter, in order to provide a pattern for our lives. We are to look at what he has done and, with great care, trace our lives over it. As one writer puts it, Jesus is '*the* paradigm by which Christians write large the letters of his gospel in their lives'.[5] He is our example.

The example of Jesus is before us, and by following it we become more like him. We learn the patience and grace which he displayed throughout his life, even to the point of death, and so we follow him through suffering and into glory. In fact, as Sinclair Ferguson has

[3] C. S. Lewis, *The Problem of Pain*, contents page.
[4] *Strom*, 5.8, as noted in Edmund Clowney, *The Message of 1 Peter* (Leicester: IVP, 1988), p. 118.
[5] Karen Jobes, *1 Peter* (Grand Rapids: Baker, 2005), p. 195.

said, 'In God's workshop in this world, suffering is the raw material out of which glory is forged.'[6]

What our suffering does for others: consolation

The Bible points to a second precious result which can flow from our suffering. It can be used in the end to bring deep consolation to others. In 2 Corinthians 1:3-4, Paul writes:

> Blessed be the God and Father of our Lord Jesus Christ, and Father of mercies and God of all comfort, who comforts us in all our affliction, so that we may be able to comfort those who are in any affliction with the comfort with which we ourselves are comforted by God.

This is a precious truth for suffering Christians. It may well be that the reason for your suffering lies before you rather than behind you. It may well be that, having been through this experience, you will be able to minister to others in the future and bring them a consolation you could never otherwise have brought. This is an astonishing achievement of God, greater than any alchemist. He pours into your life the dirt and dross of pain, and he brings out of your life the precious gold of comfort and hope.

There is a four-step pattern in Paul's thinking: we undergo affliction, receive comfort, see others undergoing affliction, and we impart comfort. It's not true that we can be of no use to someone unless we've been through exactly what they're going through. Nonetheless, there is an undeniable depth and power of sympathy which comes from the shared experience of suffering. In that sense, one of the rich resources that God has given to his church is men and women who have been through a lot. Old tears can become stagnant and bitter, but they can also become a deep well of compassion the consolation from which to draw for the benefit of others so that what comes to one as pain, comes to another as

[6] Sinclair B. Ferguson, *In Christ Alone* (Lake Mary: Reformation Trust, 2007), p. 203.

comfort.[7] Paul says: 'If we are afflicted, it is for your comfort and salvation; and if we are comforted, it is for your comfort…' (2 Corinthians 1:6). In other words, his suffering and comfort are experiences which are pointing forward and preparing him to provide comfort for those who will suffer after him. That means there will be times when others encourage and strengthen us, but are only able to do so because of the weakness and suffering which they endured years ago, and the comfort which God poured into their lives then. On the other hand, at some point in the future, through your weakness and suffering now, God will strengthen and encourage someone else. In this way the grace of God passes from one generation to the next.

There may be times when there is far more going on in our suffering than we could possibly know as we experience it. Remember the man born blind, in John 9? Where Jesus' disciples have a little philosophical debate about the cause of this suffering in his sin or his parents' sin, Jesus cuts right across their categories and speaks of a plan of God that is far bigger than they had conceived, and a purpose of God that is far grander than they had imagined: 'It was not that this man sinned, or his parents, but that the works of God might be displayed in him' (John 9:3).

Perhaps, at times, our afflictions are permitted by God – even ordained by God – so that, in six months' time, or in five years' time, or in fifty years' time, the works of God might be displayed in our lives as we become channels of his grace. That means that every ounce of affliction that you experience confronts you with a question: what will you do with your pain? What will pain *become* in your life? Will it settle there and putrefy – a festering bitterness that poisons your life and the lives of others? Or will it become a deep well of compassion and comfort – clear, cold, pure spiritual water that thirsty souls will be able to drink from in time to come?

You may have seen this yourself in people you have known. Maybe you've known someone whose life has been hard, and it has

[7] I am indebted to David Gibson of Trinity Church Aberdeen for this imagery.

destroyed them. Your heart goes out to them, but it's sad to see their bitterness and the soul-destroying anguish of regret and resentment. On the other hand, maybe you've also known an older believer who has been through much, and yet somehow all the pain has been formed into beauty rather than bitterness. What has gone in as pain has come out as wisdom, grace and godliness. The pressure of affliction, bearing down on them, hasn't destroyed them like a car in a scrap-yard crusher, but instead has acted like the intense pressure and heat that works on carbon to form it into a diamond.

It's a truly precious and beautiful thing when God puts in pain and brings out comfort – when he puts in grief and brings out grace.

What our suffering does for God: glorification

The response of Jesus in John 9 also draws our attention to a further result of suffering in the life of the Christian, namely the glorification of God. 'Jesus answered, "It was not that this man sinned, or his parents, but that the works of God might be displayed in him"' (John 9:3). Incidents like these were part of the school in which Peter learned that trials come to God's people so that the tested genuineness of their faith 'may be found to result in praise and glory and honour at the revelation of Jesus Christ' (1 Peter 1:7). The fact that God produced a faith in his people which was stronger than their trials, and the fact that they counted it a privilege to suffer for him, will result in his glorification. In some sense, beyond what we can presently know, things will actually be *better* because of the trials we've been through. Somehow, they will make glory even more glorious.

Can God use suffering to achieve good things? The follower of Jesus, who has stood at Calvary, knows the answer. It was through the suffering of his Son that God brought about our greatest joy and his greatest glory. This is the wisdom of God in the gospel, and the reason he can be trusted even when it feels like everything in life is going wrong.

Tim Keller likes to quote from a sermon by Jonathan Edwards, who would become one of the greatest preachers of the eighteenth century. It's the first sermon we have from Edwards, called *Christian Happiness*, that he preached when he was just eighteen years old. He spoke in the style of his day, but Keller has summarised the three points of his sermon by saying that, if you're a Christian, then:

- your bad things will ultimately work out for good;

- your good things can never be taken away from you;

- and your best things are yet to come.[8]

For all these reasons, we can and we must continue to follow Jesus when it hurts.

[8] Timothy Keller, *Walking with God through Pain and Suffering* (London: Hodder & Stoughton, 2013), p. 300.

CHAPTER FIFTEEN

Following Jesus Always:
The Essentials of Perseverance

And we know that for those who love God all things work together for good, for those who are called according to his purpose. ²⁹ For those whom he foreknew he also predestined to be conformed to the image of his Son, in order that he might be the firstborn among many brothers. ³⁰ And those whom he predestined he also called, and those whom he called he also justified, and those whom he justified he also glorified.

³¹ What then shall we say to these things? If God is for us, who can be against us? ³² He who did not spare his own Son but gave him up for us all, how will he not also with him graciously give us all things? ³³ Who shall bring any charge against God's elect? It is God who justifies. ³⁴ Who is to condemn? Christ Jesus is the one who died – more than that, who was raised – who is at the right hand of God, who indeed is interceding for us. ³⁵ Who shall separate us from the love of Christ? Shall tribulation, or distress, or persecution, or famine, or nakedness, or danger, or sword?

³⁶ As it is written,

> *'For your sake we are being killed all the day long;*
> *we are regarded as sheep to be slaughtered.'*

³⁷ No, in all these things we are more than conquerors through him who loved us. ³⁸ For I am sure that neither death nor life, nor angels nor rulers, nor things present nor things to come, nor powers, ³⁹ nor height nor depth, nor anything else in all creation, will be able to separate us from the love of God in Christ Jesus our Lord. – Romans 8:28-39.

Simon Peter, a servant and apostle of Jesus Christ,

To those who have obtained a faith of equal standing with ours by the righteousness of our God and Saviour Jesus Christ:

² May grace and peace be multiplied to you in the knowledge of God and of Jesus our Lord.

³ His divine power has granted to us all things that pertain to life and godliness, through the knowledge of him who called us to his own glory and excellence, ⁴ by which he has granted to us his precious and very great promises, so that through them you may become partakers of the divine nature, having escaped from the corruption that is in the world because of sinful desire. ⁵ For this very reason, make every effort to supplement your faith with virtue, and virtue with knowledge, ⁶ and knowledge with self-control, and self-control with steadfastness, and steadfastness with godliness, ⁷ and godliness with brotherly affection, and brotherly affection with love. ⁸ For if these qualities are yours and are increasing, they keep you from being ineffective or unfruitful in the knowledge of our Lord Jesus Christ. ⁹ For whoever lacks these qualities is so short-sighted that he is blind, having forgotten that he was cleansed from his former sins. ¹⁰ Therefore, brothers, be all the more diligent to make your calling and election sure, for if you practise these qualities you will never fall. ¹¹ For in this way there will be richly provided for you an entrance into the eternal kingdom of our Lord and Saviour Jesus Christ.

¹² Therefore I intend always to remind you of these qualities, though you know them and are established in the truth that you have. ¹³ I think it right, as long as I am in this body, to stir you up by way of reminder, ¹⁴ since I know that the putting off of my body will be soon, as our Lord Jesus Christ made clear to me. ¹⁵ And I will make every effort so that after my departure you may be able at any time to recall these things. – 2 Peter 1:1-15.

Introduction: praise God for the greatest Protestant heresy

Rewind five hundred years. Back in the sixteenth century, the Protestant Reformation changed the face of the Christian church forever. Many central truths of the gospel had been lost. The Bible, rather than being the supreme authority in all things, was overruled by the traditions of the church. Reformers like Martin Luther and John Calvin returned to the Bible and rediscovered great truths which had lain ignored for centuries – better news than they had ever imagined, of a more glorious God than they had ever conceived, and a more wonderful gospel than they had ever dreamed. So thrilled were they that the motto of Calvin's Geneva, and the unofficial motto of the Reformation, became *post tenebras lux*, which means 'after darkness, light'. If you go to Geneva today you can visit the *International Monument to the Reformation* in the grounds of the University of Geneva, better known as the *Reformation Wall*. It's a hundred metre long wall fronted by statues of ten great Reformation figures. Behind them, carved in stone, is their motto: *post tenebras lux*. These men felt as if morning had broken after a long night, with the darkness of mediaeval superstition and religious formalism finally swept away by the light of the rediscovered gospel. They gave themselves to the task of declaring this gospel to the world.

Of course the Reformation was not welcomed by all, and one of its staunchest opponents was a certain Cardinal Robert Bellarmine. He hated the teaching of the Reformers, but you might be surprised to discover what he singled out as the greatest theological mistake he believed they were making. 'The greatest of all Protestant heresies,' declared Bellarmine, 'is assurance.'[1]

Isn't that interesting? When the Bible was reclaimed, one of the Reformers' rediscoveries was that a Christian can know a solid assurance of enduring faith and eternal life. This particular Reformation emphasis is closely related to a doctrine known as 'the perseverance of the saints', which simply means that those who are truly saved by God can never lose their salvation. I hope you can see immediately how important that idea is for our Christian lives, and for our joy. Can I be sure that my faith will endure? I'm trusting in Christ, but can I have confidence that I will always keep

---

[1] Quoted by Sinclair B. Ferguson, *In Christ Alone*, p. 149.

on trusting in Christ and walking with him for the rest of my days, until I'm taken to be with him forever? Or is it possible – through sin, or stupidity, or senility, or anything else – for me to lose my salvation? Do I need to worry that I might fall away one day, or can I know to the depth of my soul that I am eternally saved and safe? The Reformers affirmed clearly and boldly that Christian assurance is God's desire for his people. They recognised that it's perfectly possible to make a false profession of faith, but they also insisted on the biblical teaching that no one who has a true and living faith in Christ can ever lose it.

We're going to look at this in two sections but I can't emphasise strongly enough that we're looking here, not at two different things, but at two sides of the same coin. We'll look at the issue from God's perspective, and then from ours. Looked at from God's perspective, this is about his preservation of his people. Looked at from our perspective, it's about our perseverance in faith. These are not two things, but one.

The preservation of God's people

We begin with the aspect which is more fundamental, namely God's preservation of his people. The heart of the Bible's teaching here is this: whatever it might *feel* like, in reality I am not saved from sin, death and hell because I have taken hold of God, but because God has taken hold of me. My security rests, not upon my grip on him, but upon his grip on me. Neither does my security vary from day to day, according to how well I think I am doing in my Christian life – which is why it's so important for Christians to be governed, not by their feelings, but by faith.

To borrow an illustration from the *Discipleship Explored* course, imagine you're a parent walking beside a busy road with your toddler. Cars are flying past at high speed. As you walk along the road, do you hold out a finger for your child to take hold of if they want, or do you grab their hand and never let go for anything?

The reason I can never lose my salvation is not my holding on to God, but his holding on to me. In the next few pages I want to show you that in the Bible, over and over again, and in all sorts of different ways, God makes this clear. The whole shape of our salvation proclaims that, if we are truly saved, we can never be unsaved. I'm sure there are more, but I'm going to set out ten ways in which the Bible drives this point home to us. As you read them, think about them. But most of all, feel their impact upon your soul.

Number One: if you're a Christian it's because, before the beginning of time, God chose you to be his. We can't go into the profound mysteries of election and predestination here, and how they relate to free will. These questions often arise because we simply don't understand just how big God is, but in any event this is the clear teaching of Scripture. For example, Paul tells the Christians in Ephesus to praise the God and Father of our Lord Jesus Christ because 'he chose us in him before the foundation of the world, that we should be holy and blameless before him' (Ephesians 1:4). He didn't choose us so that we should be saved, and then lost, and then saved, and then lost, depending on the constancy of our faith. God, who always accomplishes his purpose, chose us.

Number Two: if you're a Christian, it's because Christ actually *achieved* your salvation, dying for your sins and rising to put you right with God. It would have been wonderful enough if Jesus had laid down his life for the sake of the great mass of humanity, but what he did is even more amazing: he died to save you. He did all that the Father had sent him to do for his people, until his work was finished. This means that your salvation does not depend upon the uncertainties of how you might live and die, but upon the rock-solid certainty of how Jesus lived and died. What Christ accomplished by his life, death and resurrection wasn't an opportunity for you to save yourself if you trust him well enough. He saved you. He paid your debt in full, and it is gone. He achieved salvation for you and handed it to you as a free gift, including the very faith by which you receive it! It is yours, and you cannot lose it. It doesn't need to be added to, altered, supplemented, tweaked, boosted or anything else. If you need assurance of that, read the book of Hebrews. Time and time again, we are reminded of the completed nature of Christ's work and the security we can therefore have as believers. Jesus, by one sacrifice, has 'perfected for all time those who are being sanctified' (Hebrews 10:14), and so we are invited to approach God 'with confidence' (Hebrews 4:16; 10:19) and with 'full assurance of faith' (Hebrews 10:22).

Number Three: if you're a Christian, it's because God has redeemed you from slavery to sin and death. Death and hell no longer have any rights over you, and cannot claim you, because death is the wages of sin and your sin has already been punished in Christ. Because Jesus died as your substitute, the justice of God has been satisfied. The full penalty for your sin has been paid, and it can never be demanded again.

Number Four: if you're a Christian, you have been united to Jesus Christ. The Bible teaches that faith unites us to Christ forever. We are bound to him, and he is bound to us, with an unbreakable bond. Consider William Tyndale's reflection on this. His language is old-fashioned but wonderful: 'Christ is in thee, and thou in him, knit together inseparably. Neither canst thou be damned, except Christ be damned with thee: neither can Christ be saved, except thou be saved with him.'[2] In other words, because of our union with Christ, we are as secure as the Son of God! Paul goes even further, insisting that God has already 'raised us up with him and seated us with him in the heavenly places in Christ Jesus' (Ephesians 2:6). Heaven is his, and we are in him, therefore heaven is ours.

Number Five: if you're a Christian, you have been born again into a new life. The only way you can have faith in the first place is if God works within you to give you a new heart which is capable of

[2] Quoted by Michael Horton, *Putting the Amazing Back into Grace* (Grand Rapids: Baker Books, 2002), p. 253.

responding to the gospel. In fact, 'if anyone is in Christ, he is a new creation. The old has passed away; behold, the new has come. All this is from God...' (2 Corinthians 5:17-18). Do you see how God has taken hold of you, and wrought a change in you which cannot be reversed?

Number Six: if you're a Christian, you have been reconciled to God. His anger at your sin has been turned away by the sacrifice of Christ. Everything about you that made you his enemy has been dealt with by his grace. More than that, the righteousness of Christ has been reckoned to you, is counted as yours, and God therefore looks upon you as his perfect child. Reconciliation is a great New Testament theme, and a ground of confidence. God isn't like a moody teenage friend who's your best buddy, then falls out with you, then is your best buddy again, and so on. Instead, as Paul puts it at Romans 5:10, 'if while we were enemies we were reconciled to God by the death of his Son, much more, now that we are reconciled, shall we be saved by his life'.

Number Seven: if you're a Christian, you have been adopted into God's family. This is another of the New Testament's pictures of salvation, and it's a glorious one. God predestined us for adoption (Ephesians 1:5). Christ redeemed us 'so that we might receive adoption as sons. And because you are sons, God has sent the Spirit of his Son into our hearts, crying 'Abba! Father!' So you are no longer a slave, but a son, and if a son, then an heir through God' (Galatians 4:5-7). When we address God as our Father, we mean what we say, and we know that God does not abandon his adopted children.

Number Eight: if you're a Christian, you have been justified. This is important. It's a courtroom picture. To be justified means to be declared righteous. That means that God's verdict on us is in. The judgment which awaits us all one day is brought forward in the case of the believer, and the outcome is declared now. Because Christ has died for our sins and gifted his righteousness to us, there is only one possible verdict, and God tells his people now what that verdict will be. You are justified. You are free from judgment, forever.

Years ago, I used to be a court lawyer. I remember one case where the other side were (of course!) being completely unreasonable, so we ran the case in court and won. The judgment was issued, it was all over, and my client went on his way rejoicing. Then the other side had the temerity to appeal. Although (of course!) we eventually won the appeal too, it's a let-down when the appeal papers come in. You thought it was done and dusted, and suddenly you have to argue it all again. The case is reopened and it's all up for grabs before a higher court.

Justification means that God's verdict on you has been pronounced and is final. If you are in Christ, then you are, and always will be, counted righteous in him. Sin and death and Satan can accuse you all they like, but they are out of appeals. There is no higher court.

Number Nine: if you're a Christian, you have already entered into eternal life. This is immensely liberating. One of the reasons you don't have to fear death any more is that your death has already happened! You died with Christ, and rose with him, and the life you now live is one that you live by faith (Galatians 2:20). One of my favourite texts in the Bible is that glorious statement of Jesus: 'Truly, truly I say to you, whoever hears my word and believes him who sent me has eternal life. He does not come into judgment, but has passed from death to life' (John 5:24). The crucial change has already occurred. Once you have entered into eternal life, by definition, you can never lose it.

Number Ten: if you're a Christian, you have promise after promise from Jesus himself that he will keep you safe. We don't have the space to go through them all, but this is the Good Shepherd who knows and loves and keeps his sheep.

> I give them eternal life, and they will never perish, and no one will snatch them out of my hand. My Father, who has given them to

me, is greater than all, and no one is able to snatch them out of the Father's hand (John 10:28-29).

In all these ways and more, God makes it clear to us in his word that our salvation is secure. The notion that we could lose our salvation would make a nonsense of the whole New Testament, and would make Jesus into a liar. We've probably all known people who have professed Christian faith and then fallen away, but we're seeing here that in those cases the profession of faith was never real in the first place. True Christians can make all sorts of mistakes, and go far off the rails at times, but they can never finally fall. We cannot be un-elected, un-saved, un-redeemed, un-united to Christ, un-born again, un-reconciled to God, un-adopted, un-justified, un-granted new life or un-protected by Christ.

There are, in addition to everything I've mentioned, dozens of individual texts which make clear that there is no condemnation for those of us who are in Christ Jesus (Romans 8:1); that Christ will sustain us to the end, guiltless, because God is faithful (1 Corinthians 1:8-9); that we have received a kingdom that cannot be shaken (Hebrews 12:28); that he who began a good work in us will bring it to completion at the day of Christ (Philippians 1:6); and so on.

What it all comes down to is this: God loves his people with an unbreakable love. He doesn't take hold of us and let go of us, and then take hold of us again and let go of us again. He doesn't walk his children by the borders of hell and let us decide whether to hold on to him or not. He holds us! Our security rests not upon our grip on him, but upon his grip on us. It rests on his unbreakable love. If you're still looking for assurance, put this book down now and pick up your Bible and read – slowly – through Romans 8. You'll find there some of the greatest and most glorious words ever written in the history of the world.

The perseverance of God's people

Now we turn over the coin and consider the other side of the same truth. We've seen that we can have great confidence in the final salvation of all who are truly trusting in Jesus, because God has promised himself to them and has pledged to keep them forever. We called that the preservation of God's people. But what does that mean for us in our lives? What about the perseverance of God's people? Is there anything left for us to do in active pursuit of the Christian life, or do we just sit back and relax because God has taken care of it all? That was Cardinal Bellarmine's objection: if people are completely assured of salvation, what's to stop them living as they please?

By way of answer, read 2 Peter 1:1-15, and as you read it keep asking yourself the question: what kind of life does Peter look for and expect in response to God's work of grace in saving us? You'll see that Peter reminds us that God has called us to his glory, has given us precious and very great promises, has rescued us from sin and corruption, and has put his own nature within us. Then, at verse 5, he says, 'For this very reason'… what? Sit back and do nothing? No, instead he says, 'For this very reason make every effort' to live from this point forward as a believer. God has called you, therefore 'be all the more diligent to make your calling and election sure' (verse 10). In other words, when God promises his preservation, we respond with perseverance. Glory may be certain, but the path to certain glory is one of persevering faith:

> … if you practise these qualities you will never fall. For in this way there will be richly provided for you an entrance into the eternal kingdom of our Lord and Saviour Jesus Christ (2 Peter 1:10-11).

Of course, here we need to guard against making the opposite mistake, assuming it's all over to us now and we're on our own until we've persevered to the end. The point is that we keep going, not in our own power, but securely held by the hand of the God whose love will not let us go.

In a book wonderfully titled *The Joy of Calvinism*, Greg Forster says this:

> People who are truly converted to God will never fully and finally turn back because God creates in them, by the power of the Holy Spirit, a love for him that is so powerful it perseveres through all trials. If we are true Christians, our love for God is unbreakable because God's love for us is unbreakable, and his wonder-working power is always at work in us.[3]

That means that a person who is truly saved will persevere in faith. Christians can certainly experience doubt, temporary backsliding and partial falling-away. We remain sinners until we die, so these things will happen, but true faith will always endure in the end. That means that our confidence in our salvation cannot rest on a prayer that we once prayed, or a card that we once signed, or a date that we wrote in the front of our Bibles. There's nothing wrong with any of those things in itself, but they cannot be the source of our confidence. True conversion is followed, always, by a life of persevering faith in God, enduring obedience to and lasting love for God. So we look constantly to Jesus Christ, his cross, his gospel and his promises. As we do that, we persevere through all things.

Let me set out three aspects of that perseverance.

First, we persevere over the long haul.

In an age of immediate gratification, we lift our eyes to a far horizon. We give ourselves to what Eugene Peterson has so aptly called 'a long obedience in the same direction',[4] which is a good description of the life of faith. There are mountain-tops and there are valleys, but so many of our days are ordinary. The great challenge is to hand over the ordinary days to God and to make them days of obedience and faithful following, one after another after another. As Paul

---

[3] Greg Forster, *The Joy of Calvinism* (Wheaton: Crossway, 2012), p. 130.
[4] Eugene Peterson, *A Long Obedience in the Same Direction: Discipleship in an Instant Society* (Downers Grove: IVP, 2000).

David Tripp has put it, 'You live your life in the utterly mundane. And if God doesn't rule your mundane, he doesn't rule you, because that's where you live.'[5] The great privilege is that our mundane can become significant, as ordinary run-of-the-mill days are offered to God as a sacrifice of obedience to him.

Secondly, we persevere through blessing.

That might seem a strange thing to say, but many of us are living in days of such extraordinary affluence that our earthly comforts can make the things of eternity sit lightly upon us. We are distracted from them, and from the call to persevere in faith. This is a real danger, and we must take great care not to follow after the way of Demas. You can hear the sorrow in Paul's voice as he speaks of Demas in his second letter to Timothy. He had appeared to be a believer, and yet Paul urges Timothy, 'Do your best to come to me soon. For Demas, in love with this present world, has deserted me' (2 Timothy 4:9). If we are to persevere, we must not fall in love with this world.

Thirdly, we persevere through suffering.

The second part of Hebrews 10 is about assurance, holding out the prospect that we can draw near to God in 'full assurance of faith' (verse 22). Then the writer says this:

> But recall the former days when, after you were enlightened, you endured a hard struggle with sufferings, sometimes being publicly exposed to reproach and affliction, and sometimes being partners with those so treated. For you had compassion on those in prison, and you joyfully accepted the plundering of your property, since you knew that you yourselves had a better possession and an abiding one. Therefore do not throw away your confidence, which

---

[5] Paul David Tripp, 'War of Words: Getting to the Heart for God's Sake' in *The Power of Words and the Wonder of God*, ed. John Piper and Justin Taylor (Wheaton: Crossway, 2009), p. 24.

has a great reward. For you have need of endurance, so that when you have done the will of God you may receive what is promised.

There then follows the great chapter, Hebrews 11, on the heroes of faith – those who persevered – and then this, at the beginning of chapter 12:

Therefore, since we are surrounded by so great a cloud of witnesses, let us also lay aside every weight, and sin which clings so closely, and let us run with endurance the race that is set before us, looking to Jesus, the founder and perfecter of our faith....

This is the key thing. The true source of Christian assurance is a gaze that is fixed upon Jesus himself, the one who gave us faith in the first place and the one who has promised to bring it to completion.

Marriage – What's Faith Got To Do with It?

Introduction: it's complicated

In 2012, Mark Zuckerberg announced that Facebook had reached one billion active monthly users. Frighteningly, it took only a further five years for that figure to reach two billion. Through Facebook, you can tell the world all about yourself – in interminable detail, if you wish – and one of the things you can announce if you so desire is what is romantically called your 'relationship status'. A drop-down menu gives all sorts of options, one of which is: 'It's complicated.'

To some degree, if we're honest, it's always complicated. Life is complicated, people are complicated, and that means that relationships are complicated. All the signs are that it's only going to get more complicated and Christians can no longer assume, as past generations could, that people walking through the church door for the first time will share with us a basic understanding of life and a basic framework of morality. More and more, those whom Christ calls into his family will have histories and relationships that are hugely messy. We cannot abandon the clear teaching of God's word, but it's crucial that we relate to people with gentleness, patience and a great deal of grace.

Of course, some will always be deeply offended by what the Bible teaches about relationships. Many will continue to see that teaching as laughably old-fashioned and unrealistic. We would do well, however, to take heed of something Paul wrote to a group of very young Christians in Thessalonica:

> For this is the will of God, your sanctification: that you abstain from sexual immorality; that each one of you know how to control his own body in holiness and honour, not in the passion of lust like the Gentiles, who do not know God... For God has not called us for impurity, but for holiness. Therefore whoever disregards this, disregards not man but God, who gives his Holy Spirit to you (1 Thessalonians 4:3-5, 7-8).

So the question you need to ask yourself as you read the following pages is not what I think and whether you agree with me, but what God teaches in his word.

I want to set out in this chapter why I am convinced that the Bible teaches Christians not to marry non-Christians, why this issue has profound ramifications for our entire lives, and why the church in our age desperately needs to hear this.

Also, because 'it's complicated', we need to be equally careful to address another question: what if you're already married to someone who is not a believer? That can happen because we didn't know that it was wrong, because we did know but went ahead anyway, or because we came to faith in Christ after we were married. We'll address all of that shortly, but we're going to begin by addressing the question of whether a believer should deliberately marry an unbeliever, and that means I need to ask you something. If you are a Christian who is married to a non-Christian, for any reason, by any route, please bear with me while we address this. That will not be easy for you, because I cannot warn single people as I must without writing things that will be hard for you to read. Please hang in there. You might find yourself starting to wonder if what you did in your life was right. If so, remember that God loves to take our mistakes and bring out of them something new and amazing. Or you might be starting to wonder just how complex and difficult a situation you now find yourself in, having come to faith before your husband or wife. If so, remember that God is all-powerful, and promises you his grace and help as you seek to live for him.

Paul addresses the subject of marriage in 1 Corinthians 7, and it would be worth taking a few minutes to read that chapter. Here, I'm going to borrow Paul's terms of address at the beginning of verses 8 and 10 – 'to the unmarried' and 'to the married' – but we'll be looking at the Bible's teaching more broadly.

To the unmarried…

First, to the unmarried, whether you marry and whom you marry are two of the biggest questions you'll ever face in this life. For some, they may also be some of the hardest questions you'll ever face because this is an area where, sometimes, what we want collides head-on with what God says. The choice then becomes very stark: will we follow our own desire, or God's design? I have known a number of people who have professed faith in Christ but, finding themselves still single in their mid-30s, and having a deep desire to marry, have panicked. Their desire has collided with God's design, and their desire has won out. They've walked away from what they would once have said about relationships, and have married non-Christians. Some have made shipwreck of their faith as a result.

What does the Bible say? I want to look at the New Testament, and then see how that fits with the Old Testament, and then see how the teaching of the Bible makes sense in the light of our experience.

1. The lessons of the New Testament

There is no New Testament passage which specifically sets out to address the question we're asking here. That seems surprising on the face of it, and we'll consider later why that is, but for now we begin with two verses which touch on the subject indirectly.

The first is 2 Corinthians 6:14, where Paul is emphasising the difference between faith and unbelief. Stressing how incompatible they are, he commands us, 'Do not be unequally yoked with unbelievers.' Imagine a great wooden yoke, to bind farm animals together so they can pull a plough. Now imagine putting a massive ox on one side, and a newborn lamb on the other. It doesn't work. Unequal yoking leads to going round in circles, or pulling in opposite directions. In the context, Paul is not speaking specifically about marriage but about the Christian life more generally. Marriage does seem to be a particularly suitable application of the principle, but if this were all that the Bible said on the subject, I'm not sure it would be enough to make us conclude clearly that a Christian should not marry a non-Christian.

However, then there is 1 Corinthians 7:39. Here Paul says that 'A wife is bound to her husband as long as he lives. But if her husband dies, she is free to be married to whom she wishes, *only in the Lord*' (emphasis added). To marry 'in the Lord' means to marry a believer. If you are united to Christ by faith, you are to marry someone else who is united to Christ by faith. Here Paul happens to be talking about widows, but the principle would apply to all. Perhaps most telling of all is the fact that he makes no attempt to explain the reasons why a Christian shouldn't marry a non-Christian. This is more of a passing reference, as if what he's saying is already well-known among Christians and will be immediately understood when he reminds them. In my view, if this were all that the Bible said on the subject, it would be enough to make us conclude clearly that a Christian shouldn't marry a non-Christian.

In addition to these specific passages, bear in mind how insistently the New Testament teaches us of the importance of putting Christ at the centre of every aspect of our lives. It is hard to reconcile that with marrying an unbeliever.

2. The lessons of the Old Testament

When we turn to the Old Testament, we find God repeatedly warning Israelites against marrying non-Israelites. People sometimes misunderstand this as racist. God is not telling his people not to marry outside of their race, but not to marry outside of their faith. The surrounding nations followed their own gods. If they turned to the Lord they would be welcomed within the Israelite fold, but otherwise intermarriage was forbidden. The reason is set out countless times. For example:

> You shall not intermarry with them, giving your daughters to their sons or taking their daughters for your sons, for they would turn away your sons from following me, to serve other gods. Then the anger of the LORD would be kindled against you, and he would destroy you quickly (Deuteronomy 7:3-4).

Moses then goes on to make crystal clear what is at stake:

> For you are a people holy to the LORD your God. The LORD your God has chosen you to be a people for his treasured possession, out of all the peoples who are on the face of the earth (Deuteronomy 7:6).

The very identity of God's people, belonging wholly to him, depends in part upon their marrying within the faith. Marrying outside of the faith exposes us to the severe danger that we are drawn away from God and towards the worship of false gods. Today, your non-Christian husband or wife is unlikely to draw you away to the worship of Molech or Artemis, but they absolutely will draw you towards the worship of whatever it is they're worshipping in the place of the true God. It may be a lifestyle, a career, a standard of living or something else, but the priorities of husband and wife will inevitably clash. The only way to avoid constant conflict will then be for the Christian spouse to hold back from the level of commitment they could have had if they were married to a believer.

Try to understand for a moment how completely ingrained these principles were in the life of God's people. Then remember that the New Testament takes root in the culture of the Old. The earliest Christian believers were people whose entire thinking had been shaped by the Old Testament. Once you understand that, it becomes very obvious that the New Testament has little explicit teaching about this subject, not because it's not important, but because it's so obvious that it hardly needs to be said. Of course God wants Christians to marry Christians. Paul's aside in 1 Corinthians 7:39 is telling because it reveals a deep underlying assumption. It would have been inconceivable to him for a Christian to marry 'out of the Lord'.

3. The lessons of sanctified common sense

This is the biblical teaching, and it fits well with what you might call sanctified common sense. If you've followed this book's portrayal of what it means to be a follower of Christ, you should be able to see why marrying an unbeliever is such a terrible idea. We're back to the testimony of Kathy Keller which I mentioned in Chapter 9, based on twenty years of experience in dealing with this issue. 'If only,' she says.

> If only I could pair those sadder and wiser women – and men – who have found themselves in unequal marriages (either by their own foolishness or due to one person finding Christ after the marriage had already occurred) with the blithely optimistic singles who are convinced that their passion and commitment will overcome all obstacles.

She describes the frustration of counselling Christians who have already given their heart to someone to the point that they are no longer willing to listen to the Scriptures:

> Instead, variants of the serpent's question to Eve – 'Did God really say?' – are floated, as if somehow this case might be eligible for an exemption, considering how much they love each other, how the unbeliever supports and understands the Christian's faith, how they are soul-mates despite the absence of a shared soul-faith.[1]

---

[1] Kathy Keller, 'Don't Take It from Me: Reasons You Should Not Marry an Unbeliever', https://www.thegospelcoalition.org/article/dont-take-it-from-me-reasons-you-should-not-marry-an-unbeliever. Accessed 18 April 2018.

To the unmarried, I need to say this as clearly as I can. To be a Christian means to have Jesus Christ at the very centre of your life, informing every thought you have and directing every decision you make. That is what it means to say that Jesus is Lord. If you marry an unbeliever, then you are binding yourself to someone who is thinking and deciding in fundamentally different ways. It doesn't work. It's like yoking together a massive ox and a little lamb and expecting them to plough a straight furrow.

Maybe, like me, you know of one or two situations where a believer has dated or married an unbeliever and, in time, that unbeliever has come to faith in Christ. That is not evidence that this is a good policy, but rather that we have a good and gracious God who works despite the mistakes of his people. We should never presume upon his grace. It's fairly common to hear this argument from Christians who want to date or marry non-Christians: 'Oh, but you never know, they might come to faith.' Paul himself uses the 'you never know' argument in 1 Corinthians, but he uses it to make exactly the opposite point. He addresses a situation where someone has become a Christian and their spouse separates from them.

> But if the unbelieving partner separates, let it be so. In such cases the brother or sister is not enslaved. For how do you know, wife, whether you will save your husband? Or how do you know, husband, whether you will save your wife? (1 Corinthians 7:15-16).

The notion that a believer can marry an unbeliever in the hope that they might come to faith later is not to be found anywhere in the Bible.

Finally it should also be clear that, if you're not going to marry a non-Christian, you shouldn't date a non-Christian. When you date someone, you mess with their heart. You also walk into a minefield of temptation yourself. So even at the level of dating, unequal yoking goes against God's ways. It also exposes a deeper fallacy in our thinking and a deeper problem in our hearts. As a Christian, how do you decide who you might be interested in dating in the first place? In Alistair Begg's book on marriage, his first criterion for a woman looking for a husband is that 'The man should be committed to growing in his relationship with Christ'; and his first consideration for a man looking for a wife is that 'A good wife must have personal faith and trust in the Lord Jesus.'[2] Far too many Christians have allowed the unbelieving world to shape their thinking on this, so that physical appearance is the main or only factor. I'm not saying we should marry people we find unattractive, but I am questioning what we find attractive. We need to be asking different questions. Is this a godly person? Is he mature in faith, so that together we will explore the joys of salvation and deepen our relationship with Christ? Is she someone who is committed to the Lord, so that instead of two people negotiating their competing agendas in life, we will pursue God's agenda together? Is this a person of true Christian character; someone who will face life with strength and grace; someone in whom God is at work; someone with whom I want to grow in faith and hope and love? Past generations understood this. Thomas Boston, a great Scottish preacher of the eighteenth century, was first attracted to his future wife because he 'discerned in her the sparkles of grace'.[3]

Tim Keller paints a wonderful picture of a Christian couple who stand at the front of a church knowing that one day they will stand before the Lord. Their shared prayer is that, on that day, they will hear God say:

> Well done, good and faithful servants. Over the years, you have lifted one another up to me. You sacrificed for one another. You held one another up with prayer and with thanksgiving. You confronted each other. You rebuked each other. You hugged and you loved each other and continually pushed each other toward me.[4]

That, and nothing less, is a worthy vision for Christian marriage.

[2] Alistair Begg, *Lasting Love* (Chicago: Moody Press, 1997), pp. 52, 60.

[3] Andrew Thomson, *Thomas Boston: His Life and Times* (Fearn, Ross-shire: Christian Focus, 2004), p. 51.

[4] Timothy Keller, *The Meaning of Marriage* (London: Hodder & Stoughton, 2011), p. 123.

Of course at this point it's possible that you're thinking this is all well and good, but there are simply no suitable Christians in your church or social circle who could become a spouse for you. What if, for you, faithfulness means singleness? We don't have space here to address this issue with anything like the care that it needs, but we need to be clear that the word of God remains the word of God whatever its implications for us might be. We also need to debunk the cultural myth that singleness is a dreadful, lonely fate. We need to be clear that a single life lived in faithfulness to God, while it might have its sorrows, is infinitely preferable to a married life lived in defiance of God. For those to whom singleness is unwelcome and unwanted, please let me encourage you to stand fast in your obedience. There may be times when this feels like an almost unbearable burden, but it is not. God sees your faithfulness, and he will walk with you each day with grace sufficient, and he will reward your obedience. For now, keep on loving Jesus enough to submit this part of your life to him too.

To the unmarried, God says: if you marry, marry one of my people.

To the married...

To the married, the message is equally important. If you are a believer married to an unbeliever, please don't think I'm suggesting that your marriage is not valid or valuable, or that you've made a mistake which is not redeemable. God is rich in grace. He knows that we can't go back and undo what we have done, and given the sacredness of marriage he would not want us to.

1. To those who knew

Of course, there are different routes to a mixed marriage. In some cases the believing partner did what they did knowing it to be wrong, or at least not stopping to surrender the decision to Christ as they should have done. If you were a believer at the time of your marriage and you knowingly married an unbeliever, then I need to say that what you did was wrong and the first thing you need to do is repent. That may be one of the most important steps in seeing God redeem the situation you're now in. It doesn't matter whether your spouse has since come to faith or not: you need to repent.

Having done this, you need to be assured of the free grace of God. That sin, once repented of, is gone forever. You will live with the consequences of it, as we'll discuss shortly, but the guilt of it is wiped away for good.

2. To those converted later

For others, you're in a mixed marriage because you have come to faith since you were married. At the time of your wedding neither of you were believers, but since then God has drawn you to himself. That is cause for great rejoicing and thankfulness. God has done two things: he has shown great mercy towards you, and he has established a foothold for the gospel in your family. Your situation is now one of challenge and opportunity.

The challenge is that some of what we described earlier will happen in your life. If Christ is Lord of your life, then your priorities and desires will start to be shaped by him. As you grow in faith and become more familiar with God's word, your thinking will change. You will find, over time, that you and your spouse don't think about things in quite the same way any more. That will be difficult, both for you and for your spouse, who may feel threatened by your new commitment to Christ.

The opportunity is that God has placed you where you are for a reason. The life of Christ now lives in you, to shape you and empower you for his service. You will have a greater influence than anyone else over your spouse and children. Through you, there is the opportunity for the message of the gospel to reach them powerfully. When Paul wrote to Timothy, who was a young pastor, he gave a fascinating glimpse into his home background: 'I am reminded of your sincere faith, a faith that dwelled first in your grandmother

Lois and your mother Eunice and now, I am sure, dwells in you as well' (2 Timothy 1:5). Later, Paul adds:

> But as for you, continue in what you have learned and have firmly believed, knowing from whom you learned it and how from childhood you have been acquainted with the sacred writings, which are able to make you wise for salvation through faith in Christ Jesus (2 Timothy 3:14-15).

Paul makes no mention of any Christian man on the scene, but two godly women nurtured the young Timothy in faith. If you are the first in your family to trust in Jesus, you never know what God might be doing through you. You may become the beginning of something new in your family. There may be generations to come who will thank God for the day he took hold of you, because through you the gospel came to many. You may feel entirely inadequate for that, but he is more than able to do it.

3. To all

Regardless of how you came to be married to an unbeliever, one thing is clear: anyone who has truly grasped the gospel will long for the salvation of their loved ones who are not yet Christians. This is your husband or wife, and you love them, and you long for all that is good for them. As a believer you recognise that their greatest need is to know Christ as their Saviour and Lord.

What does all of this mean in practice? It means you will need great wisdom from God to know how best to share the gospel with your husband or wife. You will need insight to determine how much of the gospel can be shared at any one time, and in what way. You will need great sensitivity and insight concerning the confusion which the change in your life may bring about in them. You will need to be praying constantly that the Lord would show you how to express your wholehearted commitment to him while being sensitive to the needs of your not-yet-believing spouse. You will need great grace from God to live a life which commends the gospel. You will need courage to pray for opportunities to share the gospel, and boldness for the moments when God answers those prayers.

These things are not easy, but what a sense of potential there is once God is at work in a family. Be encouraged. Remember that you are only a Christian because God opened your blind eyes. Pray, every day, that he would show the same grace to your husband or your wife.

4. To everyone

The existence of 'mixed marriages' is likely to become more common in our post-Christian culture. If you are not in one, be a friend and encourager to those who are. Above all, pray for them. We're all one family, having been given a relationship status that we do not deserve: we are sons and daughters of the living God. This God is still in the business of adding to his family, and building his church. So even as we trust in his power, let's do everything in our power to ensure that our husbands and our wives become part of this greatest of families.

APPENDIX TWO

Suffering – Where Is God When It Hurts?

Introduction: why?

On 15 February 1947 a young man called Glenn Chambers was about to fly from Miami to Ecuador, where he planned to work as a missionary. While waiting at the airport, he decided to write to his mother before he left. Having nothing to hand, he picked up a scrap of paper in the airport terminal. It was an advert from a newspaper, with a single word in the centre of the page but blank space around it. He quickly scribbled a note around the edges, posted it and boarded the flight. The plane crashed into a mountain in Colombia, and all the passengers and crew were killed.

The news of his death reached his mother – followed, the next morning, by the envelope that he had posted. She opened it to find his note to her, written around the edges of that one huge word in the middle of the advert. The word was: 'Why?'[1]

The existence of suffering, particularly in its more extreme forms, is one of the most common objections raised against the Christian faith. Any attempt to 'solve' the problem of pain is inevitably trite, so our aim here is more modest: I want to offer

---

[1] Charles R. Swindoll, *The Finishing Touch: Becoming God's Masterpiece* (Dallas: Word, 1994), pp. 170-171.

some perspectives which are important in a Christian response to the issue.

Suffering and belief systems: where is atheism when it hurts?

We need to begin by considering suffering and belief systems, because the question of how to make sense of suffering is not exclusive to Christianity. It applies to any belief system, and it arguably applies most devastatingly to atheism or agnosticism. Why do I say this?

There are two questions that can be asked about suffering. The second is, 'If God exists, why is there suffering?' We'll come to that. But there is also a first and prior question which people ask instinctively, regardless of their beliefs. It's that most basic question that we've already seen: 'Why?' Not 'Why would God allow this?', but just 'Why is this happening?' It is deeply significant that human beings react to suffering in that way. We want to know why. We look for a purpose or a meaning. All by themselves, our hearts rise up within us and cry out, 'Why is this happening?' That question drives us, not away from God, but towards him.

After all, within an atheistic view of the world, there is no reason for anyone ever to ask that question. Why should we ask why? Why should we look for a reason? Why should suffering seem wrong at all? In a purely naturalistic view of the universe, in which the physical world is all that exists, human beings are simply part of nature red in tooth and claw. If you've ever watched nature documentaries, you'll know that nothing could be more 'natural' (in a fallen world) than violence, pain and death. So why do we cry out against it? On what basis can we complain about it, or expect anything better? To be an atheist – at least a consistent one – you have to accept that suffering is normal and isn't really a problem. This is just our lot. A meaningless universe delivers up meaningless pain, and we do our best to anaesthetise ourselves with meaningless pleasure. This is life. Anything else would be an anomaly, which is why arch-atheist Richard Dawkins wrestles so agonisingly with the inconvenient truth that 'We humans have purpose on the brain.'[2] He just can't understand why we ask why. This is what he said once in a newspaper interview:

> Suppose that some child is dying of cancer, we say; 'Why is this child dying; what has it done to deserve it?' The answer is, there's no reason why… there's no reason other than a series of historical accidents which had led to this child dying of cancer. No reason to ask why.

When the interviewer pointed out that, nonetheless, people do ask why, the only response Dawkins could offer was, 'That's their problem.'[3]

It's not easy to tell a grieving parent that God is real and loves them intensely, but is it any easier to tell them that there's nothing wrong with what's happened to them at all? Will they be comforted by the knowledge that the death of children is just a normal and natural part of life? Will it stop them asking why this has happened? This is what we're left with, in the absence of God. It's legitimate to ask the question: where is atheism when it hurts?

The fact that suffering feels so wrong suggests, not the absence, but the existence of a God who has designed life with purpose and meaning. The atheist has to ask: if I am the chance product of a mindless evolutionary process, and if there is no good design to which human life is meant to conform, why do I know in the midst of my pain that something is not right? Why do I feel to the depths of my soul that this is not as it should be?

Far from allowing us to escape the problem of pain, atheism only raises deeper problems. But we still need to consider why we can and should trust in a good God with a loving purpose, even in a world racked with suffering.

[2] Richard Dawkins, *River Out of Eden* (London: Weidenfeld & Nicolson, 1995), p. 96.
[3] *Daily Telegraph*, 31 August 1992, quoted in John Blanchard, *Does God Believe in Atheists?* (Darlington: Evangelical Press, 2000), pp. 551-552.

Suffering and creation: how did it all begin?

The fact that we experience suffering as an anomaly – not the way things should be – makes perfect sense within a Christian world-view. The Bible says very clearly that this kind of experience of life is not what we were made for. God did not design human beings to suffer and die.

In the Bible's account of creation, every time God creates anything, he looks at it and sees that it is good. Finally we read that, having created human beings and charged them to look after the earth, 'God saw everything that he had made, and behold, *it was very good*' (Genesis 1:31, emphasis added). In the beginning, human beings did not suffer. God, people and the natural world all had their rightful place, and everything was interrelated just as it should be. Life was just right. That perfect existence is what we were designed for, and that design is built into us.

So this is our first Christian perspective on suffering: the reason it feels wrong is that it is wrong.

Suffering and the Fall: symptoms of a fatal disease

If suffering is not the way God designed things to be, what is going on? The problem, according to the Bible, is that something has gone badly wrong, and it has to do with our attitudes and actions towards God. We'll start with the conclusion, and then look at how we get there. The conclusion I want to take from a Christian writer who says this: 'The word "suffering" would not exist if man had not shaken his fist in his Creator's face.'[4] The problem is that, although God created us to live in harmony with him and in happiness, we have sought to dethrone him and live our own way. The Bible refers to this as the Fall. The first human beings rebelled against the God who had given them everything, and without exception we have all done the same. We have sinned.

[4] John Blanchard, *Does God Believe in Atheists?* (Darlington: Evangelical Press, 2000), p. 537.

The Bible explains that human sin has consequences for the whole of life. Imagine black ink poured into a basin of water. It doesn't just affect the water molecules it hits, but spreads through everything. In the same way, the whole of human life is affected by the stain of humanity's rebellion against God. As a human being I have a physical body, a mind and a spirit or soul. I live in a physical environment. I inhabit a social environment, through my relationships with others. Because of sin, all of this has been disrupted and damaged in ways that cause me pain. Bad things don't necessarily happen to me as a direct punishment for my own sin, but in a more general sense the sinfulness which has infected every human being has had an impact in every sphere of life. Our bodies develop diseases, and ultimately they die. Our minds also malfunction, think wrong thoughts, and degenerate. Our souls or spirits, which should be directed towards God, become twisted in upon themselves. Our social environment is affected, so that our relationships are damaged. Our physical environment is affected, as the whole world around us feels the effects of selfishness and sin. This may be the hardest aspect to grasp – how humanity's sin can affect nature itself – but the Bible speaks about the earth itself being cursed and the whole creation being frustrated. In some ways this is much easier to comprehend than it used to be. A great deal of suffering in some of the poorest parts of the world is caused by what we like to call 'natural disasters' or even 'acts of God', but which we're increasingly coming to understand are the result of our own mistreatment of the planet. That fits amazingly well with what the Bible has been saying for thousands of years.

Is this a comprehensive and completely satisfying explanation for individual instances of suffering? Of course not. But is it relevant to the question of how a perfect God relates to suffering? I think it is. Suffering is a sign that there is something terribly wrong with the human condition. This is exactly the way our bodies work: pain is hugely valuable in alerting us to the fact that things are not as they should be. Dr. Paul Brand, a Christian who has spent his life working with leprosy patients, tells of an occasion when he fell ill and returned home by train. As he undressed, he became aware that he had no feeling in his left heel.

> I lightly pricked a small patch of skin below my ankle. I felt no pain. I jabbed the pin deeper, longing for a reflex, but there was none – just a speck of blood oozing out of the pinhole. I put my face between my hands and shuddered, longing for pain that would not come.

Brand spent the rest of the night imagining his future life with leprosy.

> Dawn finally came, and I arose, unrested and full of despair. I stared in a mirror for a moment, summoning up courage, then picked out the pin again to map out the affected area. I took a deep breath, jabbed in the point – and yelled aloud. Never has a feeling been so delicious as that live, electric jolt of pain synapsing through my body. I fell on my knees in gratitude to God.[5]

Brand realised that, sitting on the train for a long period the previous day, he had numbed a nerve in his leg leading to temporary loss of sensation in his foot. It reminded him why he has so often said that, if he could give his leprosy patients one gift, it would be the gift of pain. The great curse of the condition is the absence of pain, alerting the sufferer to the fact that there is something wrong which needs to be addressed. Only pain tells us that, and only pain is insistent enough to make us pay attention.

In a very important sense, we need suffering. If life doesn't hurt, how are we to know that it's broken and needs fixed? Pain is a sign that something has gone wrong.

[5] Philip Yancey and Paul Brand, *Fearfully and Wonderfully Made* (London: Harper Collins, 1987), pp. 124-127.

Suffering and eternity: the promise of something better

So is there no hope? Are we just doomed to suffer? The Bible says no, and our next perspective is that of suffering and eternity. Since suffering was not God's design for us, but is an alien intrusion telling us that something is badly wrong, God has told us in his word that this is not what will finally be.

There are two stages to the undoing of suffering. First, we need to recognise in the life of Christ the promise of something better. Read any of the gospels and you will see Jesus beginning to reverse all the effects of human sinfulness which I mentioned earlier. Our bodies have broken down, but Jesus heals. Our minds have been disrupted, but Jesus restores them. Our spirits have malfunctioned, but Jesus turns people back to God and makes it possible for them to live in relationship with him. We are subject to death, but Jesus raises the dead. Our physical environment has been damaged, but Jesus exercises total authority over the elements. Our relationships have broken down, but these are signs of the breakdown of our deepest relationship with God himself. This is what Jesus came to heal.

So we watch as Jesus begins to undo the effects of sin in the world. It's only a beginning, but what an intimation of the possibility of something better!

The second stage of this biblical perspective on suffering is to consider the stunning promises of God about his purposes for eternity. He will complete what Jesus began. He will put right all that is wrong. He will end suffering, completely and forever, for all who trust him. The Bible pictures what will happen at the end of time, when a loud voice in heaven says:

> Behold, the dwelling place of God is with man. He will dwell with them, and they will be his people, and God himself will be with them as their God. He will wipe away every tear from their eyes, and death shall be no more, neither shall there be mourning nor crying nor pain any more, for the former things have passed away (Revelation 21:3-4).

I certainly don't want to suggest, in trite fashion, that suffering doesn't matter because it will end one day. Those who suffer, or who watch helplessly as others suffer, know that it does matter. But is there not also a danger of losing perspective in the opposite direction, as if the present moment of suffering is all that exists? The Christian needs to see the suffering of this life against the background that your existence as a human being does not last for sixty or seventy or eighty years, but for eternity to come. When Paul wrote to Corinth, neither writer nor recipients were strangers to suffering, and yet he reminded them that 'this slight momentary affliction is preparing for us an eternal weight of glory beyond all comparison' (2 Corinthians 4:17). It's not that it doesn't hurt. It's just that we need to remember the eternal joy which lies before us as God's people.

Suffering and redemption: the significance of the cross of Christ

One further, inescapable perspective on suffering is provided by the Bible's explanation of how God achieves this final victory over suffering in the redemption that Christ wins. God himself takes our suffering upon himself. He comes in the person of Christ, and willingly endures greater suffering than you or I ever will. He does this for our healing and release.

> Surely he has borne our griefs and carried our sorrows... he was wounded for our transgressions; he was crushed for our iniquities; upon him was the chastisement that brought us peace, and with his wounds we are healed (Isaiah 53:4-5).

This is where Christianity is different from any other belief system in the world. No other faith has a suffering God. They have strong gods, or impassive gods, but not suffering gods. Other religions approach suffering in different ways. Endure it. Embrace it. Find serenity in it. Transcend it. Ignore it. Deny it. In Christian faith we find something utterly different. We find God incarnate hanging on a cross, God-in-human-flesh being physically undone in the cruellest execution. Surely, again, this is significant? A suffering world cries out to God, appeals to God, accuses God – only to discover that he is himself a suffering God.

In his great book *The Cross of Christ*, John Stott reflected on this:

> I could never myself believe in God, if it were not for the cross.... In the real world of pain, how could one worship a God who was immune to it? I have entered many Buddhist temples in different Asian countries and stood respectfully before the statue of the Buddha, his legs crossed, arms folded, eyes closed, the ghost of a smile playing round his mouth, a remote look on his face, detached from the agonies of the world. But each time after a while I have had to turn away. And in imagination I have turned instead to that lonely, twisted, tortured figure on the cross, nails through hands and feet, back lacerated, limbs wrenched, brow bleeding from thorn-pricks, mouth dry and intolerably thirsty, plunged in God-forsaken darkness. That is the God for me! He laid aside his immunity to pain. He entered our world of flesh and blood, tears and death. He suffered for us. Our sufferings become more manageable in the light of his. There is still a question mark against human suffering, but over it all we boldly stamp another mark, the cross which symbolizes divine suffering.[6]

Does that solve the problem and answer all our questions? No. But is it relevant? I think so. I think it does go some way towards explaining how it's possible for a good God to co-exist with evil and suffering. It also has great significance for our sufferings in that, if God went into ultimate suffering for us, surely he is in our suffering with us? The point is not that the cross tells you why you have cancer. The point is that the cross tells you that you can trust God even when you have cancer.

Suffering and faith: where does trusting God come into this?

That brings us to the final perspective I want to offer on suffering, which is the place of faith. I want to suggest that what we really need in suffering is not ultimately a reason, but a relationship.

[6] John Stott, *The Cross of Christ* (Leicester: IVP, 1989), pp. 335-336.

Most people today misunderstand what faith is. Faith is what you're left with when you have no evidence or rational basis for asserting something. When all else is gone, then you just have to have faith. The truth is that faith simply means belief or, better, trust. In the Greek in which the New Testament was written, 'have faith', 'believe' and 'trust' are all one word – because throughout the Bible, the essence of faith is not believing a statement or a doctrine but trusting a person. Often that does involve trusting them for things we don't know and can't prove for ourselves, and in that sense faith goes beyond what we ourselves can understand. However, believing something because you trust someone is a long way from believing something just because you've taken a fancy to believe it.

Neither is there anything essentially religious about faith. We all exercise faith all the time, including atheists. On the basis of what we do know, we trust people for what we don't. We know, for example, that airlines don't take in vagrants off the street and ask them to fly their planes. We know that they train their pilots rigorously and that there are all sorts of safety procedures. This is why, even though we've never met the man sitting in the cockpit, and we don't know him from Adam, and he could be a plumber for all we know – and even though our lives are at stake – we get on the plane. Do you see what's happening? We're trusting. We're making an informed judgment, but that informed judgment is inescapably a step of faith. On the basis of what we do know, we're trusting someone for what we don't know.

Is that irrational? Of course not. We all trust people all the time for things we don't know. The only question is: is our trust well-placed? Or, to put the question another way, is the person we're trusting trust-worthy?

The Bible never pretends to answer the philosophical problem of pain. It gives important perspectives on it, as I hope we've seen, but it doesn't give easy answers. It does tell us, however, that God gave up his Son for you and me, to die for our sin, so that we can enjoy eternal glory and happiness with him. The person who has faith in Jesus Christ therefore responds like this: 'I may not fully understand why there is so much suffering in this world. I may be uncertain of many things, but my settled conviction is this: God sent his Son to die for my sin. I know this. And so, on the basis of what I know, I can and will trust him for what I don't know.'

Is there an easy answer? No. But I want to suggest that an easy answer is not what we need. We need to know that God is with us in our suffering, and we need to know that God can be trusted to see us through our suffering. This is what we need – and in Jesus Christ, this is what God gives us.

Recommendations for Further Reading

Every topic we have explored in the chapters of this book deserves a great deal more space than I can give it here. So for each chapter I'm recommending below one book which you might like to read if you want to go into further detail.

1. Faith

Ian Hamilton, *The Faith-Shaped Life* (Edinburgh: Banner of Truth Trust, 2013)

2. The Bible

Kevin DeYoung, *Taking God at his Word: Why the Bible Is Worth Knowing, Trusting and Loving* (Nottingham: IVP, 2014)

3. The Church

Matt Chandler, Josh Patterson, Eric Geiger, *Creature of the Word: The Jesus-Centered Church* (Nashville: B&H Publishing, 2012)

4. Prayer

Eric J. Alexander, *Prayer: A Biblical Perspective* (Edinburgh: Banner of Truth Trust, 2012)

5. The Holy Spirit

David Jackman, *Spirit of Truth: Unlocking the Bible's Teaching on the Holy Spirit* (Fearn, Ross-shire: Christian Focus, 2006)

6. Holiness

J. C. Ryle, *Holiness: Its Nature, Hindrances, Difficulties and Roots* (Edinburgh: Banner of Truth Trust, 2014)

7. Growth

J. I. Packer, *Growing in Christ* (Wheaton, IL: Crossway, 2007)

8. Guidance

Phillip D. Jensen and Tony Payne, *Guidance and the Voice of God* (Kingsford: Matthias Media, 1997)

9. Relationships

Christopher Ash, *Married for God* (Nottingham: IVP, 2007)

10. Parenting

Timothy Sisemore, *Our Covenant with Kids: Biblical Nurture in Home and Church* (Fearn, Ross-shire: Christian Focus, 2008)

11. Evangelism

John Chapman, *Know and Tell the Gospel* (New Malden: Good Book Company, 1998)

12. Work

Sebastian Traeger and Greg Gilbert, *The Gospel at Work: How Working for King Jesus Gives Purpose and Meaning to our Jobs* (Grand Rapids: Zondervan, 2014)

13. Stewardship

R. C. Sproul, *How Should I Think About Money?* (Sanford: Reformation Trust, 2016)

14. Suffering

Timothy Keller, *Walking with God through Pain and Suffering* (London: Hodder & Stoughton, 2013)

15. Perseverance

Michael A. Milton, *What is Perseverance of the Saints?* (Phillipsburg: Presbyterian & Reformed, 2009)

Appendix 1: Marriage

John Piper, *This Momentary Marriage* (Nottingham: IVP, 2009)

Appendix 2: Suffering

Michael Baughen, *The One Big Question: The God of Love in a World of Suffering* (Farnham: CWR, 2010)

The Faith-Shaped Life
Ian Hamilton

The Christian life is a faith-shaped life. Faith is the instrument that
unites us to Christ, but it is also the reality that shapes how we live in
union with Christ. From beginning to end the Christian lives by faith.

In this book Ian Hamilton shows that the life of faith is not easy.
The Christian is engaged in an unrelenting warfare with the world,
the flesh and the devil. Every step forward will be contested. The
one thing that will keep the believer on track and pressing on is
moment by moment trust in God, in his word, in the goodness
and perfection of his purposes, and in his exceedingly great and
precious promises. 'This is the victory that has overcome the
world—our faith' (1 John 5:4).

ISBN 978 1 84871 249 2 | 160 pp. | paperback

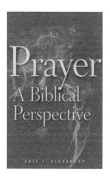

Prayer: A Biblical Perspective
Eric J. Alexander

Prayer matters, and Eric Alexander's chief concern in this book
is to remind Christians that prayer is fundamental, and not
supplemental, both in the individual and in the corporate lives
of God's people. He shows that nowhere is this dependence on
prayer more fully exemplified than in the life and teaching of Jesus
himself, and in the ministry of the New Testament church.

Church leaders will find these studies a great spur to pray for the
spiritual growth of their people, and church members will see
afresh the urgent need to pray for their leaders.

ISBN 978 1 84871 149 5 | 106 pp. | paperback

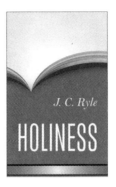

Holiness
J. C. Ryle

This book is perhaps J. C. Ryle's best-known and, arguably, best-loved book. Although many things have changed since 1877, when this book was first published, one thing remains the same: 'real practical holiness does not receive the attention it deserves'. It was to remedy this attention deficit, and to counter false teaching on this most important subject, that Ryle took up his pen. The twenty-one chapters in this enlarged edition highlight: the real nature of holiness, the temptations and difficulties which all must expect who pursue it, the life-transforming truth that union with Christ is the root of holiness, and the immense encouragement Jesus Christ holds out to all who strive to be holy.

ISBN 978 1 84871 506 6 | 480 pp. | paperback

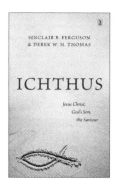

Ichthus: Jesus Christ, God's Son, the Saviour
Sinclair B. Ferguson & Derek W. H. Thomas

Ichthus is the Greek word for a fish. Its five Greek letters form the first letters of the early Christian confession that 'Jesus Christ is the Son of God and Saviour'. To draw a fish sign meant: 'I am a Christian.'

To be a Christian, according to the New Testament is to know Christ. But who is he, and what is the meaning of his life? In *Ichthus*, Sinclair Ferguson and Derek Thomas answer these questions by taking us on a tour of nine key events in Jesus' life and ministry. Their aim is to help us both understand and share the confession made by those early Christians.

ISBN 978 1 84871 620 9 | 184 pp. | paperback

About the Publisher

The Banner of Truth Trust originated in 1957 in London. The founders believed that much of the best literature of historic Christianity had been allowed to fall into oblivion and that, under God, its recovery could well lead not only to a strengthening of the church, but to true revival.

Interdenominational in vision, this publishing work is now international, and our lists include a number of contemporary authors, together with classics from the past. The translation of these books into many languages is encouraged.

A monthly magazine, *The Banner of Truth*, is also published, and further information about this, and all our other publications, may be found on our website or by contacting either of the offices below.

THE BANNER OF TRUTH TRUST

3 Murrayfield Road
Edinburgh, EH12 6EL
UK

P O Box 621, Carlisle
Pennsylvania 17013
USA

banneroftruth.org